Leading While

BLEEDING

OVERCOMING OBSTACLES THAT CAN HINDER YOUR SUCCESS

How To Heal From The Hurts And
Pains of Leadership

ANTHONY AND MICHELINE MCFARLAND

Published by

Harvest Publishing
PO BOX 6249
Altadena, CA 91001

Leading While Bleeding

ISBN-13: 978-1543292992
ISBN-10: 1543292992

Editor: Flo Jenkins – Words That Flo!...
Editorial Consultancy Services (goodjenksmedia@gmail.com)
Art Director: Anthony McFarland
Cover Design: Anthony & Micheline McFarland

TABLE OF CONTENTS

DEDICATION

This book is dedicated to every leader, couple, and volunteer who is on the front lines of ministry or leading companies; those who have been through the fire, through the storms of life, family, business and ministry, and found themselves bleeding while leading. It is dedicated to those who have been judged, misunderstood, and criticized by people in and outside of your ministry or family. We believe that God can heal and stop your hurt or emotional pain (bleeding). He can do it for you ... but it takes *work*!

My wife, Micheline, and I want to thank every present and past member of the Abundant Harvest LIFT who have loved us, taught us in a very unique way, and those who have left us the right or wrong way— you all have helped us grow, shift, and transform into the leaders we are today.

To our daughters, Amika and Jessica, we love you dearly. What a journey it has been for all of us as we have experienced the ups and downs of family pains, purposing to love each other and grow through every challenge we have faced and confronted over the years.

To the leaders and partners within the Kingdom of God International, each of you have made a special impact in and on our lives; we will be forever grateful.

To mother Sheila Ferguson, who transitioned to be with the Lord God Almighty in 2018: I/We thank you for always bringing things to my attention when you sensed something was off, wrong or not right, and pulling me to the side to have that mother-and-son talk. Thank you for calling me aside to confront and correct things that needed to be addressed, whether it was about me (my attitude or something I said), or regarding my marriage, family or ministry affairs. You were a great confidant and counselor to us both! You will be forever missed by the masses and every child you helped throughout the years who was bleeding and had no one to care about them!

It is our prayer that this book will be like a First Aid Kit that helps leaders from all walks of life. My desire is that it especially helps God's Fivefold gifts and Helps Ministry volunteers (*kings and priests*) recognize if they are bleeding and how to deal with it. This is so that they may experience the healing that is required to fulfill their kingdom assignment on this journey called faith! And, for those who take a position that you never bleed, we love you and are praying for you; but maybe this book can help you to help someone stop bleeding and leaking all over themselves and others around them to the point of self-destruction.

Wherever you are in this journey of faith, just know that God wants us all to be WHOLE in Christ in order to fulfill our kingdom assignments on whatever mountain He has placed you, so that you bring Him much glory!

INTRODUCTION

This book is written for individuals who have gone through many heartfelt hurts and life challenges while in leadership positions. Leading and not dealing with the onset of pains and disappointments can cause many malfunctions while leading. Your position as a leader while bleeding from past hurts can create unnecessary conditions with you and with others. As a leader, you are in the position of influence and can have good or bad effects on those around you.

My wife, Micheline, and I may know a little about this; we've been married almost 30 years. Micheline once had a thriving business for years, and she was very successful at it. We are now leading together in our church and have been in this position for the past 19 years. What we have learned is that you can lead while bleeding and not know it. We have seen this from many personal experiences and have witnessed many of our friends, family, and peers even die in that state. We've come to realize that it is crucial that you do the work and deal with matters; otherwise, it can cost you dearly.

> *Denial keeps people in inertia, whereas acknowledgment and acceptance are necessary for bringing about change.*

There are many leaders with visions and dreams; yet those aspirations appear to be far reaching, and no matter what you do, nothing seems to happen for you. You can work for years and nothing is fruitful or productive.

Because of these disappointments, many things can happen; you can open up wrong doors that allow wrong spirits to enter—and you can even get sick as a result of this undealt with pain or internal bleeding.

There is a saying that, "Sin will take you further than you want to go, keep you longer than you want to stay, and cost you more than you want to pay." In this book, we are using the term 'bleeding' in the context meaning *hurt*, *offenses, unforgiveness, betrayal, backbiting,* and *fits of rage.*

James 5:13–16 (KJV):
13: Is any among you afflicted? let him pray. Is any merry? let him sing psalms. 14: Is any sick among you? let him call for the elders of the church; and let them pray over him, anointing him with oil in the name of the Lord: 15: And the prayer of faith shall save the sick, and the Lord shall raise him up; and if he have committed sins, they shall be forgiven him. 16: Confess your faults one to another, and pray one for another, that ye may be healed. The effectual fervent prayer of a righteous man availeth much.

As Christians, we know that applying biblical principles to our lives will give us a stronger foundation. We know this, but what are we doing about it? In other words, what makes a good, healthy leader, or a leaking leader? One who knows how to apply the Word of God and walk by faith under extreme mental and emotional warfare.

A perfect example is when I first came into ministry and had my first experience with combat. I almost failed because I did not know how to handle the hurt and disappointment. We had just obtained our first church building, and literally months later, we received a letter from the City stating that the building was not zoned for church use, because we were in an industrial area. I now had to inform the members that we had to move out of the new location after raising $20,000 and spending a little over $18,000 on the building.

When we were having services in a hotel, my wife and I told people that, "Our first building will be just as nice as the Double Tree Hotel and the Armenian Cultural Center we had services in last year." Now, we had to contact the owners to address a lease agreement and be faced with losing money and finding another space.

The biggest hurt, however, was having to go and tell these faithful members that the City had informed us that we must *move*, after spending all of the money on a building we were all so proud of. I tell you, the fear of not knowing how the people would respond was extremely unnerving.

Despite the fear, we chose to walk in a level of faith and trust in God. We decided *not* to allow the situation and circumstance to get the best of us; such as me responding with bleeding (hurt) and crying. To my surprise, that would not be the first and last encounter we would have with a building. Wait until I share with you in another chapter the experience that hurt, cut me to my core, and scared me to the point that I wanted to seriously hurt someone!

We have watched so many leaders over the years fail to recover from a disappointment over an attack that would lead them to a deviating course, because they did not know how to handle the challenges that come along with leadership and success.

I remember several years ago, a news report stated that mortgage giant, Freddie Mac's chief financial officer, killed himself after discussing a possible resignation. In April 2009, the

Washington Post reported that Freddie Mac's acting CFO, David B. Kellermann, had talked about resigning from his post before hanging himself on a piece of exercise equipment. The 41-year-old had been having disagreements over disclosures to investors and faced mounting stress over an impending SEC filing, the *Post* reported.

The sad commentary to this story is that, "the chief human resources executive spoke with David earlier that week and suggested David take some long-deserved time off with his family," said David Palombi, a Freddie Mac spokesman. "At no time was he asked to resign, and at no time was there any suggestion that his duties would be diminished."

It's clear that he could not handle the pressure of failing as a leader and did not know how to stop the internal thoughts that caused him to bleed to the point of suicide. Kellermann's body was found by his wife, Donna, in the basement of their home in the Hunter Mill Estates subdivision in Vienna, according to law enforcement sources. He had hanged himself on a piece of exercise equipment, the sources said. How sad is that!

A few years later, a dear brother we knew, who has since transitioned, went through a similar situation. He was a musician and praise leader who became very hurt by his Pastor for shutting down the music department for a season. Instead of weathering the storm and working things through, he became offended, hurt, and left the church. He took a position at another church; this time as a Pastor.

While leading and not dealing with his personal issues (demons), he started bleeding and **hemorrhaging** on others. We all know that hurt people hurt people. As a result of not dealing with his prior condition (trauma), it stirred up unaddressed internal darkness as he continued leading while bleeding, ultimately hurting his family and many people in his church. He ultimately died suddenly!

Of course, this type of bleeding will have an adverse effect on people around you and ultimately their outlook on church, because you, as a leader, don't know how to handle the warfare or distractions that come with ministry.

Jer. 2:13:
For my people have committed two evils; they have forsaken me the fountain of living waters, *and* hewed them out cisterns, broken cisterns, that can hold no water.

When you don't give attention to the root of your pain, you can turn to many ways to cover it up and find many ways to sedate yourself with things like drugs, alcohol, affairs, porno, a mean, controlling spirit, rebellion against God's authority, lying, cheating—it goes on and on. There are many detrimental escape routes you can take when you don't deal with your pain. But we must do the work by *confronting* the various issues we will personally face or have not dealt with emotionally in our assignments.

A special note was shared with me by a therapist on our pastoral staff: To suffer hurt doesn't always mean you're bleeding. Emotional hurt, such as anger, fear, anxiety, bitterness, divorce, and frustration are things that affect the soul (Ego). We all know that to bleed means a trauma may have occurred, either internally or externally.

The only time when bleeding doesn't occur externally is when there is a brace. Bracing is bleeding that occurs internally (hurt), but it may never express itself externally. On the other hand, hemorrhaging/bleeding is a physical manifestation that cannot be contained internally, but must express itself on the outside. Bleeding will normally express itself in a traumatic way.

Professional psychiatrists believe that there are 17 conditions associated with bleeding: depressed mood, emotional detachment and flashbacks, which cause you to glaze over your past heartaches, rejection, failure and hardships. Tragic things can happen when you don't take your emotional health as seriously as your physical health.

In this book, we refer to unaddressed hurt, pain, anger, bitterness, and unforgiveness as signs of bleeding.

ONE:

It's Time to Stop Bleeding!

Listen, my brother, sister or leader: If we don't know how to handle warfare of the assignment, or relationship conflict that causes hurt and pain, it will cause cracks in your armor.

Spiritual Warfare is active war waged by Satan along with his followers, such as demons and evil principalities, as they attack, thwart, harass, and mislead the followers of Jesus Christ. It is a war because these evil forces use vigorous tactics and strategies to try to stop the work of God. The enemy wants to prevent your ministry or church from functioning the way God intended it to.

The fact is, the more you make an impact for God, the more the devil—or just people who are jealous and envious are going to fight you. The enemy sows weeds in the middle of the church staff and volunteers. The reality is, you never outgrow weeds/evil spirits. It just gets more intense. If there were no devil, why would God send His Son to fight what does not exist?

If you get hateful and full of bitterness with small things, how can God promote you to bigger things? Never forget, God will promote you to the level of your tolerance of pain!

I read a blog from a leader who stated the following:

"I haven't been posting recently...as I am on my way to recovery ... yet, just recently, I find myself becoming extremely emotional and spewing it out on people. Especially when I heard that the owner of my building is selling the property. Realizing that we will have to move our church.

"But now, the bleeding of the emotions is nearly killing me...the feelings and the guilt and 'what ifs'... it's the strangest sensation when I came across this thought. Once I thought it through, I realized that it is what it is, and I have been suffering all my adult life from people who I feel abandoned me or the assignment."

There is a war going on inside of us in the natural and in the spiritual realm. The enemy sets the stage, but we have to figure out what role we are playing and how we are acting (responding) to what's going on.

The Bible says God sent Jesus Christ to defeat the works of Satan. The Bible says that Satan is the prince of this world. Jesus said so. He never disputed Satan's right to work all across the world. The Bible says in 1 John 3:8, "The Son of God came for this purpose: to destroy the devil's work".

God never called you to do ministry alone or fight alone. David recognized that when he fought Goliath. Jesse sends David on an errand to see how his sons Eliab, Abinadab and Shammah are doing. Jesse loads him up with supplies for his brothers and *"ten cheeses for the captain of their thousands"* (I Samuel 17:17-18).

Upon David's arrival, he heard the words of Goliath and saw that all the men of Israel fled from the armies of the Philistines. He was ready to fight, after all, he killed the lion and the bear to save his sheep, so what was this uncircumcised Philistine to him! David was speaking out of the inward work of God. But his brothers didn't believe in him and said he was in pride. Sometimes that's how it is in ministry or business; there will be people who question you, question your motives or who will simply be critical of you, and that can be painful.

They apparently had no recollection of, or didn't take seriously, the anointing of the Prophet Samuel. You may be anointed for your assignment, but trust me, there will be those who oppose your assignment—this includes even those you love and those you have even fought for.

Let's look at what happened with Jehoshaphat in the middle of extreme warfare. Jehaziel reminded Jehoshaphat that he was not alone! (2 Chron. 20:15). God is our warrior. He always has been and always will be our shield and buckler.

Sometimes, if we are to succeed and win a victory, the Lord has to be the One to fight the battle. This is the way it must be to win the victory over sins. Only through what God has done can we win the victory. We have no price we can offer. That battle must be the Lord's!

"So, Judah gathered together to seek help from the LORD; they even came from all the cities of Judah to seek the LORD. Then Jehoshaphat stood in the assembly of Judah and Jerusalem, in the house of the LORD before the new court, and he said, 'O LORD, the God of our fathers, are You not God in the heavens? And are You not ruler over all the kingdoms of the nations? Power and might are in Your hand so that no one can stand against You.'" (2 Chronicles 20:4-6).

An alliance of Moab, Ammon and others had invaded Judah. It was *a matter of mathematics*; the enemy by far outnumbered the people of Judah. There seemed to be only one possible outcome: the defeat of Judah.

Jumping up, Jehoshaphat stood in the temple and prayed. There was only one place to turn. Sometimes life is like that. And with reference to death, and eternity, God is the *only* One who can make a difference!

The Lord responded through His prophet, Jahaziel. ...and he said, "Listen, all Judah and the inhabitants of Jerusalem and King Jehoshaphat: thus says the LORD to you, 'Do not fear or be dismayed because of this great multitude, for the battle is not yours but God's.' (2 Chronicles 20:15).

Yes, here was a case where the battle had to be the Lord's, or it would be lost. However, just because the battle was the Lord's did not mean that the people of Judah were to sit and do nothing. They were instructed: "You need not fight in this battle; station yourselves, stand and see the salvation of the LORD on your behalf, O Judah and Jerusalem.' Do not fear or be dismayed; tomorrow go out to face them, for the LORD is with you." (2 Chronicles 20:17).

They went out and faced their enemy, and the Lord gave them victory as they watched their enemy's alliance fall apart and the former allies attack one another.

There will be times that all you need to do is yield to God, trust in God, fast and pray, and not allow your feelings to get involved in the process of fighting the good fight of faith!

It is not we who overcome the world in our own strength. We do not have a power plant inside ourselves that can overcome the world. The overcoming is the work of the Lord Jesus

Christ, as we have already seen. There can be a victory, a practical victory, if we raise the empty hands of faith moment by moment and accept the gift. "This is the victory that overcometh the world." God has promised, and the Bible has said, that there is a way to escape temptation. By God's grace, we should want that escape!

Every leader should know and understand that God's people are not the enemy. Paul was equally clear that we do not wrestle against flesh and blood. Even when people frustrate and anger us, they are not the enemy. When we remember this truth, we will love, shepherd, and pray for people differently.

> *When you have an "us and them" mentality, the devil has duped you!*

We should also know that any level of leadership is a primary target for the enemy. That truth shouldn't surprise us. The enemy knows that when leaders fall, followers are wounded in the process. I doubt I need to spend time listing the prominent Christian leaders who have fallen in the last few years.

We are to have a life filled with purpose, power, and distinction. God has separated you for your assignment and graced you with a special grace for your ministry. If we are hurting and bleeding, we will bleed out or become empty in life, becoming no good to ourselves, our family, or our ministry.

If you don't build yourself up in your most Holy Faith and continue to pursue the face and voice of God, you cannot receive the strategy required—nor can you grow—again becoming of no value to our neighbors or to God. We can try to clean ourselves up and apply purpose to our lives by our own will, but if it is not from God, it is useless. It will just invite chaos and strife into our lives.

> *Growth is never easy and never comes without pain! Next level comes with stretching and sometimes injuring a muscle!*
> *-- Anthony McFarland*

...Don't Fight Your Battle Alone! ...
...Don't Die on the Hill All by Yourself!...

Sometimes leaders must stand alone, but too often they have no close team (or other leaders) around them to help them win spiritual battles. Loners are by nature vulnerable to attack and defeat. I also want to share with some of you that when you feel alone like I felt earlier in ministry, don't allow the enemy to tell you God doesn't love you, or play the self-talk game, saying you "have done everything perfectly, and this should not be happening to me".

Listen, my friend, if you think that walking in the path of righteousness will ultimately spare you from fighting sadness, moments of insecurity, conflict, loneliness, or even outright failure, that spirit or voice doesn't ring true with what Scripture says. I know this for a fact.

Consider Jeremiah 29:11 – one of the most widely memorized and cherished verses in all of Scripture. "'For I know the plans I have for you," declares the Lord, 'plans to prosper you and not to harm you, plans to give you hope and a future.'" The thing is, at the time the prophet Jeremiah said this, he was delivering a devastating message to the Israelites that they would remain exiled in Babylon for the next several years. They would remain in captivity. Their suffering would continue. They wouldn't be receiving the get-out-of-jail-free card for which they'd been praying.

What if Jeremiah had scrapped this big bummer of a message out of fear or discomfort? After all, he already had a rep for being a "Debbie Downer"—with some people even wanting to kill him for his pessimism!

"Uh, God ... I hear what you're saying, but I'm just not really feeling at peace about all of this. I'm going to assume you want me to figure out a Plan B, because there has GOT to be a better way."

Fortunately, Jeremiah knew better. So, he faithfully shared his bold message, thereby helping instill God-grounded confidence in the hearts of those he led. You see, my dear brother or sister, Jeremiah and the Israelites were exactly where God wanted them to be.

You are exactly were God wants you. God loved them, and He wanted what would be best for them in the long run, just as He does you. He wanted them to find their hope and joy in Him on a daily basis, trusting Him regardless of their circumstances.

God's unfailing love and power make a difference in the lives of every one of His children? Consider that His power is directed by His love, and what His love motivated Him to give for us. Understand and comprehend that He is a God with whom all things are possible.

He is not limited by our lack of imagination, creativity, vision or power.

Do you recall the ancient nation of Israel, after witnessing God's power in many ways; the ten plagues on their Egyptian masters, their deliverance at the Red Sea; water from the rocks of the wilderness and food from the sky; how that nation still, tragically, lacked confidence in God's power as they stood on the brink of the promised land of Canaan (Numbers 13-14)? God was able, but they were *unwilling to believe.* God would have given them whatever they needed to win the victory, if only they had believed.

That was then, *now is now.* We find ourselves in a very similar circumstance, and that is not by accident. The Lord caused the account of Israel's lack of faith to be recorded and preserved so that we might learn not to do likewise; "Now these things happened to them as an example, and they were written for our instruction, upon whom the ends of the ages have come." (1 Corinthians 10:11)

God would have blessed them with whatever strength they would need. He will do so for us as well. Sometimes we are in the storm or difficult circumstances, and God will bring us out if we have the trust and humility to submit to Him.

You put a bandage on a cut or take antibiotics to treat an infection, right? No questions asked. In fact, questions would be asked if you *didn't* apply first aid when necessary. So why isn't the same true of our mental health? We are expected to just "get over" psychological wounds — when as anyone who's ever ruminated over rejection or agonized over a failure knows only too well that emotional injuries can be just as crippling as physical ones. We need to learn how to practice emotional first aid.

****

True Story of an Anonymous Leader
Real Life Story/Real Lessons

One pastor shared how during his time in seminary, he took a leadership course taught by a great theologian. He states, "As we studied the life of David, the professor shared a study he conducted with a group of men in full-time ministry who had fallen into a morally disqualifying sin."

At the time, I had only been a Christian for a few years, but unfortunately, the subject was all too relevant. During my early days, I had witnessed several men whom I loved and respected fall into serious sinful compromises. At one point in those days, the falls came so frequently, I felt as if I was on the spiritual beach of Normandy watching buddies' lives get blown apart all around me.

The professor's study was of 246 men in full-time ministry who experienced moral failure within a two-year period of time. As far as he could discern, these full-time clergies were men who were born again followers of Jesus. Though they shared a common salvation, these men also shared a common feat of devastation; they had all, within 24 months of each other, been involved in an extra marital affair.

After interviewing each man, the professor compiled 4 common characteristics of their lives.

1. None of the men were involved in any kind of real personal accountability.

2. Each of the men had all but ceased having a daily time of personal prayer, Bible reading, and worship.

3. Over 80% of the men became sexually involved with the other woman after spending significant time with her, often in counseling situations.

4. Without exception, each of the 246 had been convinced that sort of fall "would never happen to me."

As I reflect on this study, a few lessons come to mind. These are applicable for pastors, plumbers, stay at home moms, and anyone else who seeks to follow Christ.

Sin Thrives in Isolation.

Satan lives in the darkness and longs to keep us there as well. He does this because lies live best in the darkness. God knows this, which is why when He calls us to Himself, He calls us into the Church.

God has created the Church to be many things, one of which is to be a community of people who help each other fight sin and love Him. He calls us into relationships where we speak truth to one another (Ephesians 4:15, 25), confess sins to one another (James 5:16), and love each other enough to chase after each other if we stray (Matthew 18:10-20; Galatians 6:1-2; James 5:19-20).

The question I want you to ponder is this: Who knows you? I mean, who really knows you? Who not only has permission, but is currently acting upon the permission to ask you penetrating questions? Are you answering those questions honestly, or are you hiding details and painting up your sin to guard your image?

Do not hide from God's gracious aid of loving relationships.

Never forget the promise of God, and always prophesy His Word over your life, family, and ministry! When you pass through the waters, I will be with you; and when you pass through the rivers, they will not sweep over you. When you walk through the fire, you will not be burned; the flames will not set you ablaze. Isa. 43:2

Do the work by taking the following steps:

1. Pay attention to emotional pain — recognize it when it happens and work to treat it before it feels all encompassing.

2. Redirect your gut reaction when you fail.

3. Monitor and protect your self-esteem.

4. When you feel like putting yourself down, take a moment to be compassionate to yourself.

5. When negative thoughts are taking over, disrupt them with the WORD immediately.

6. Understand that LOSS is a part of life, but it can scar us and keep us from moving forward if we don't treat the emotional wounds it creates.

7. Know that when God or people remove themselves, they weren't meant to stay on the journey with you.

8. Face the reality that anyone who abuses and devalues is no longer necessary in your life. Don't allow the disqualified to rent space in your head or lose sleep over cancerous spirits.

9. Don't let excessive guilt linger. Yes, sometimes you're the one who blows it and hurts people, so ask God and those you've hurt to forgive you, and keep it pushing.

10. Pay attention to yourself and learn how you, personally, deal with both common and shocking attacks that cause emotional wounds.

Wisdom Nuggets:

Whenever you come to a place that you don't want to ever again experience pain, offense, and people hurting you, you are saying, "I no longer want God to expand me!" None of us enjoys being hurt. Most of us, honestly, are not steadily operating at the spiritual level that, when pain hits us, we will welcome it for the growth it will bring. However, when that pain and heartrending disappointment hits us, if we can just learn and *practice* to simply <u>pause—take a deep breath before reacting</u>; be still for a moment, and *immediately* take that hurt to the Lord.

He will calm us, and give us clarity, a deep revelation on the issue. And often, we will come away so much wiser, so much more at peace, and so much more compassionate and forgiving of those who've wounded us. (After all, but for the grace of God, we could be that person who hurts. We do know, too, that hurt people hurt people.)

Don't allow your pain to *weaken* you to the point that you allow it to block your next level! God has given you a grace to grow and go to the next level.

Don't keep going through things without *growing* through the storms of life. Pull down the wisdom, power, and strategic thinking required for your next level of greatness!

TWO:

Bleeding & Leaky People

For My people have committed two evils: they have forsaken Me, the fountain of living waters, to hew for themselves cisterns, broken cisterns, that can hold no water. - Jeremiah 2:13

Those of us not raised on a farm or a ranch might not know that a cistern is just an underground container to catch and hold water. In this verse, God mentions two of the specific ways the nation of Israel had disobeyed him. He tells them they had forsaken him, the true God, and they were trying to satisfy themselves instead of relying on him.

In Bible lands, a cistern was an artificial reservoir that was dug in the earth or hewn in the rock for the collection and storage of water. Cisterns were very important in the land of Israel because of the long dry season and the relatively few natural springs. But a broken cistern was practically worthless. Cracked rock or crumbling masonry could hold only a small quantity of dirty water, or no water at all. Collecting and storing water in a broken cistern was about as smart as carrying a sieve for a canteen!

It's like this: We're hopelessly lost in the desert, dying of thirst, seeking anything to quench our parched, dry throats. We see a kiosk with big flashing neon lights, and God is holding up a sign that says, "Living Water Available Here." Yet, we say, "No, thanks, God! Appreciate the offer, but I see a shovel over there. Think I'll dig my own cistern!"

Off we trot to start digging our own well and our own cistern. We abandon God — who doesn't just have water, but a *spring* of water that will never dry up — and decide to figure our problem out by ourselves.

The problem is our cisterns always break; they never hold up. Various hurts and voids internalized *always cause fractures to the vessel.* The water leaks out, so we remain thirsty, unable to quench our own thirst.

Jeremiah used the illustration of broken cisterns to point out the extreme foolishness of God's people, Israel. This illustration was not just thought up by Jeremiah as "sermon filler." The Lord Himself originated and used this illustration in the message that He communicated to His people through His prophet, Jeremiah (vs 1-2 and 4-5). The message was spoken as a rebuke to people who were no longer totally committed to their God. Certainly, the broken cistern sermon has an application for God's people today.

For many of us, no matter if you're a pastor, bishop, secretary or volunteer, spiritual healing will be a process. And, honestly, it wouldn't be fair of me to tell you that these three steps are easy-peasy, that healing will happen overnight, or that you'll never receive any more wounds.

Pay Attention! If a feeling of rejection, hurt, failure, or bad mood is not getting better, it means you've sustained a psychological or spiritual wound and you need to treat it ASAP!

For example, loneliness can be devastatingly damaging to your psychological and physical health, so when you or your friend or loved one is feeling socially or emotionally isolated, you need to take action.

I can tell you that, though it may take longer than we'd like, through God's grace and mercy, it is possible to have our once-and-for-all healing. Here are the steps we all must take:

Clean the Wound

If we confess our sins, He is faithful and just to forgive us our sins and to cleanse us from all unrighteousness. 1 John 1:9 (NKJV) As with any physical wound, spiritual wounds must be thoroughly cleansed in order to allow complete healing. And that can really be a painful process.

Our cleansing *starts with prayer*. We must come to Him, earnestly asking in faith that He heal us and make us whole. And we must be willing to receive our healing.

Though most spiritual wounds are caused by others, we ourselves can be the cause of our spiritual damage. No matter the cause, *unforgiveness* is at the root. We must ask God to help us forgive those who've hurt us (even if that means asking Him to help us forgive ourselves).

Guard the Wound

He heals the brokenhearted and binds up their wounds. Psalm 147:3 (NKJV)

Just as I bandaged my son's wound for protection from germs and things around him that could do further harm, spiritual wounds must be guarded from outside forces that would slow or stop the healing, and even cause more injury. While trusting that God is doing His part to bind up our wounds and ultimately heal us, we can help by vigilantly protecting our wounds. How?

> *By pushing the reset button by the renewing of your mind.*

Observe the Wound

Be sober, be vigilant; because your adversary the devil walks about like a roaring lion, seeking whom he may devour. *1 Peter 5:8* (NKJV)

Similar to a physical injury, when our spiritual wounds aren't closely monitored, we run the risk of infection. There's actually no difference when it comes to *infection*. Infection can quickly spread to the rest of our lives, poisoning our faith and our relationship with Him and with others. When this happens, we're destined for more of the same—more chronic spiritual wounds and the inability to experience liberty in Christ.

If not monitored and if you are not honest with yourself, you will start bleeding all over again on yourself and those around you.

> *Last but not least ...*
> *Trust the Great Physician for Healing.*

THREE:

Self-Examination

Do you know how to tell if you're bleeding? In this section, we have identified some of the common traits hurt people display in their interactions with others. Often, those around them become the recipients of harsh tones and fits of rage or just plain old spewing discontent with their co-workers, boss, leaders, and members in the church. That is because they have unknowingly become the vicarious recipients of transferred offense and anger.

Hurt people interpret every word spoken to them through the prism of their pain. Because of their pain, ordinary words are often misinterpreted to mean something negative towards them. As a result of this, they are extremely sensitive and act out of pain instead of reality. Never even consulting the Holy Spirit on what was just said or asking for spiritual discernment with whatever took place.

For those people who are always leaking or oozing with complaints, it is almost impossible for them to think on things which are so lovely and of good report of people, because their perception of someone has been tainted.

Q: Is that you? Are you constantly bleeding out your emotions about people, the church, family or situations that you're faced with?

Nearly every month, I talk with someone who tells me they have been "hurt by the Church". I sit in the barbershop and listen to people with flawed perspectives on the Church or leaders, because someone (a friend) has leaked flawed perspectives or bleed on them as a result of being hurt or offended by something that happened. Every time I hear these words, my heart breaks because I know exactly what they mean—and exactly what they *don't* mean. Most people's perception of a situation is flawed, and they don't exercise the Word when it comes to dealing with conflict.

> *Everyone will not value and appreciate you, the gift you are, so don't take offense! Remember, over 2,000 men walked away from Jesus in one day!*

Several years ago, my wife and I went through one of the most painful experiences in our lives. A close friend and minister hurt us deeply. Their fall resulted in a serious effect on a few members. Sadly, some people had the audacity to think *we* were the reason the person was no longer there, not knowing full details of what happened and how we had NOTHING to do with why the person betrayed their family and God. We did not publicly expose this person's sin, but instead, we concealed the matter, based on our agreement in a private meeting. As a result of not exposing the sin, in some respects, it backfired on us. Initially, I wanted to go before the congregation and reveal everything that this person had done to his family *and to us*—but I didn't.

Then, in another season of ministry, we lost people who once called us their family, because we lost a lot of money due to a property deal gone bad after much labor and monies were raised. Thereafter, opinions abounded and next they were gone, because they either perceived things a certain way or allowed unhappy others to persuade them to get on their boat and leave, too.

My wife and I felt like it wasn't supposed to be like this. We didn't believe these kinds of things were supposed to happen to us, because we were trying to do everything both right and righteous with integrity; but, somehow, things still went wrong. We trusted and loved these people and believed that they trusted and loved us. They invested in us, and we invested in them and their families. We were serving side by side in the church. Then, it seemed like in a blink of an eye, everything changed, and people were gone.

What was interesting about each of these situations is that we took it personal. We did not realize that each situation was bigger than us, and it was an opportunity for us to grow; but yet, in hindsight, it revealed a weakness. What is always interesting in some cases when people leave churches or get a divorce from their spouse, they think the grass is greener on the other side, only to find out that no one, no marriage, and no ministry is perfect! Everyone has something to work on, and wherever you go, you will encounter conflicts, misunderstandings, and even offenses.

I will never forget sitting in my car on one occasion, talking to God and crying unpleasant and hurt tears by myself ... crying out to God, asking "WHY?" So, when someone tells me, "I was hurt by the Church", I know exactly what they mean. I have been hurt, too, by members, volunteers, and other leaders who I respected. That's why it can be dangerous to be leading and bleeding all at the same time.

My prayer is that you would not be like some of the leaders I know who continue to stay in denial to their state of mind and heart condition.

I believe to speak of being hurt by "the Church or by the People" is a safe way of speaking about our pain, whether it's in private or with people we don't know. It allows us to keep a safe distance from the events that have wounded us—because "the Church or the People" is a faceless entity.

I'll never forget the time I met a pastor from Florida named Dr. Nathaniel Hill; he had brought his outstanding choir from Florida on tour and decided to make our church one of his stops. After he returned home, he called me and asked if he could share something personal with me. I said, "Of course, please share."

He said to me: "I really like you and think you have a really good ministry, but you're hurt and bleeding. I was so shocked that he would say that, but it was true, and it caused me to take another look at myself. Today we are great friends with him and his wife.

I did not realize that bleeding people interpret every action through the prism of their pain. Leaders don't realize that, oftentimes, their emotional pain causes them to suspect wrong motives or evil intent behind other people's actions in the church. That's why you see leaders who are hurt often alienate others and wonder why no one is there for them when they are in need. By their self-destructive behavior or sermons, they often continually hurt the ones they love and need the most.

That was me for a season, and it affected my marriage and ministry. I have learned over time that hurt people have the emotional maturity of the age they received their (un-dealt with) hurt. For example, if a girl was raped by a man when she was 12 years old, unless she forgives that man and allows Christ to heal her heart, her emotional growth will stop. Even when she reaches her later years, she may still have the emotional maturity of a 12-year-old.

Hurt people are often frustrated and depressed because past pain continually spills over into their present consciousness. In many instances, they may not even be aware of why they are continually frustrated or depressed. They have coped with pain by compartmentalizing it or layering it over with other things over time.

I have been in situations with people in which there was a gross overreaction to a word someone spoke or an action that was taken. It appeared that this reaction came "out of left field". But it was really the person reacting to an accumulation of years of built up hurt and pain that spilled over in various situations.

I have been in situations where I felt hurt, troubled, or overreacted to something. This is because it touched a nerve because of a wound I received in the past. In these situations, I have attempted to reason through the situation as objectively as I can. I've done this with much prayer and introspection, so I would not say or do anything damaging to another person or myself.

A minister should not preoccupy himself with making things happen or changing people. He or she should walk in integrity and humility. He or she should allow God to open up doors, deal with people, and provide greater opportunities; otherwise, you fall victim to drinking out of the wrong cistern. For clarity, I am not saying don't confront things or people, but leave room for God to do His part.

Whether it is because of a marriage problem, member issues, co-worker or continual personal conflicts with other volunteers, God often allows conflict and spillover. He wants the infection to stop spreading and the person to be healed.

Often Christians are fighting the devil and blaming him for conflict, and it's really *them*. God often allows conflict so that people will be motivated to dig deeper into their lives and seek Him. They need the help of the Lord to deal with *root causes* of destructive thought and habit patterns.

God's purpose for us is that we would all be conformed to the image of Christ (Romans 8:29). This does not just happen with Bible studies, prayer, and times of glory. It also happens in painful situations when we have to face what has been hurting us for many years.

Rarely is a person ready or even *willing* to deal with and face pain when they hit their senior years (sixties or older). Most at this age have already become hard-hearted, and/or become so depressed even though God is able to help them at any age. That's where we get the saying and even the movie, *Grumpy Old Men*.

> "*Refuse to become a victim of your circumstances or failure and give a lift to your potential each and every day against the fear of any obstacle you encounter!*"
> — Israelmore Ayivor

You see, wounded people need to pardon people from their mistakes in order to be released and restored to freedom. The Gospel of John 20:23 says that we have to release the sins of others if we are going to be released. This means that if we do not forgive others, then the very thing we have become victimized with will become a part of our life.

For example, alcoholic fathers breed alcoholic sons if their sons do not forgive and release their fathers. The good news is that, through the efficacious blood of Christ, we can all be healed. We can be set free from all past hurts. This is so that we can comfort others with the same comfort we ourselves have received from God (2 Corinthians 1:4)

Wisdom nuggets on how to protect yourself from getting hurt in church by people:

All of us hold unrealistic expectations of people from time to time. In fact, the biggest unrealistic expectation is that people shouldn't have unrealistic expectations. "Unrealistic expectations are potentially damaging because they set us and others up for failure," said Selena C. Snow, Ph.D., a clinical psychologist in Rockville, Md. When we or someone else naturally falls short, we draw false conclusions, feel negative feelings, and act in a negative way.

> *"My soul, wait silently for God alone,*
> *For my expectation is from Him"*
> *(Ps. 62:5).*

The definition of disappointment is *"the failure to attain one's expectations."* Don't expect things from the church or the minister that they can't deliver, or that the Bible doesn't teach that they should do. The first step in relinquishing unrealistic expectations is being able to spot them. This isn't always easy, especially if we've held these expectations for years.

Examples and signs of unrealistic expectations:

- "Every member must like me." The reality is that we can't make everyone like us — no matter how hard we try or how great you serve.

- "People in the church should be fair." This also is unrealistic, because we "can't control all aspects of the people or family to ensure that they operate consistently in the most fair manner."

- "My golden years were supposed to just be golden." There are many transitions and challenges in older age.

- Unrealistic expectations assume a level of control that we don't actually have in a situation. God never called for you and me to control people through our emotional needs simply because we expect them to be a certain way towards us.

41

Maybe there are some leaders like me who feel repeated disappointment that the expectation hasn't been met from those you work with in the ministry, because they fail to meet up to your standards or way of doing things. Many expectations have to do with preconceived "traditions" that we have come to associate with a church, perhaps from another church we once attended or grew up in, etc.

It's a good idea to meet with people you work with in ministry and discuss their expectations and yours. Ask them what they expect of you and you tell them what you expect of them in ministry or relationships.

> *"Do not place your trust in words of people! Trust no one but God! Then learn how to trust God with people!" -- Anthony McFarland*

Isaiah's society was similar to ours: "No one calls for justice, nor does any plead for truth. They trust in empty words and speak lies; they conceive evil and bring forth iniquity"

(Isaiah 59:4). Jeremiah warned: "Behold, you trust in lying words that cannot profit." (Jeremiah 7:8). The world is full of lying words given by the inspiration of the devil. How do I know they are lying words? *Because they contradict the Word of God!* "Indeed, let God be true but every man a liar" (Romans 3:4).

When the world tells you the lie that there is no God and that intricate life just evolved by chance, believe God, the Creator of all things, Who holds man accountable.

When the world tells you the lie that easy divorce is a good solution to marriage conflicts, believe God, who says marriage is for life and that divorce and remarriage is adultery. Seek a marriage partner who trusts in God.

"Thus says the LORD: Cursed is the man who trusts in man and makes flesh his strength, whose heart departs from the LORD"
(Jer. 17:5).

Come to terms with the fact that everyone is human and will fail you at some time or another. Even the pastor or deacon will make mistakes. The only one you can trust entirely *without fail is God.*

There's a difference between "love" and "trust." It's possible to love and forgive someone, without placing an absolute trust in them. To illustrate this, let's say there's a school bus driver who has a drinking problem. One day while transporting a load of children he becomes intoxicated, wrecks the bus and kills all the children.

As the lone survivor of the crash, he turns to the church to seek God's forgiveness for this horrible act of irresponsibility. If he repents of his sin, will God forgive him? Absolutely. Should the church love and forgive this person? Of course. And what if he would then like to volunteer to drive the church bus for us? Do we trust him? Absolutely not!

It would be unthinkable to put a person in the driver's seat who has shown such recent negligence.

Certainly, we love and forgive him, but because of this man's poor track record, we could not risk the lives of our passengers or members. Over a long period of sobriety and safe driving, this person may be able to prove that he is again reliable or trustworthy.

There was a minister we got to know before we started our church; he was a recovering drug addict who had a powerful testimony. He asked my wife and me to be a part of an advisory board for a new partnership he was forming with two other gentlemen for a men's recovery home. Unfortunately, and to his own demise, they placed him in charge of the medications and contraband that was retrieved from the men when they process them into the home.

Well, needless to say, it wasn't even a year before he was back on drugs and out in the streets. We found out a few years ago that this brother, God rest his soul, was found in an abandoned vehicle with a needle in his arm. He overdosed and died.

Remember that love and forgiveness are granted unconditionally, *but trust must be "earned".* Trust is the acquired confidence in a person's actions. We certainly can, and should trust persons who show trustworthy behavior, but because all men have the potential for failure, *we should never put an infallible sense of trust in anyone but God.* Especially those we know who possess certain weaknesses or have been challenged with certain things in their life. Remember, don't take a kid into a candy store who has a sugar addiction and think he or she won't touch or take any candy.

At the same time, we must treat others the way we want to be treated. This is the golden rule. The core message of nearly every significant spiritual text. It's the foundation upon which political ideologies and laws are built.

It's very simple in theory. If everyone followed it, laws would be unnecessary. Quality of life would skyrocket for everyone. We can all objectively agree that the more people who follow this philosophy, the better the world we live in becomes. But how many people do you know who actually make a true effort to practice it in real life?

If we all believe it, why don't we all do it?

"Therefore, whatever you want men to do to you, do also to them, for this is the Law and the Prophets." (Matt. 7:12).

Human beings tend to be "reciprocal" creatures. That is, they reflect the way they are treated. This is why Jesus gave us the Golden Rule: "Do unto others as you would have them to do unto you." The way that most people interact with you is as a direct result of how you interact with them. If you have a frown on your face, you won't get many smiles. If you offer friendliness, it will usually be offered back (Proverbs 18:24).

Be gracious, encouraging, and a blessing for others to be around. If you have a negative, critical attitude toward people, it will tend to generate their critical attitude toward you. "Judge not, and you shall not be judged. Condemn not, and you shall not be condemned. Forgive, and you will be forgiven." (Luke 6:37).

Many hurt feelings can be avoided if we will realize that people usually react to how we deal with them. Take a close examination at the way you say things, or even how much you talk. "...a fool's voice is known by his many words". Don't be rude and impolite. Check your attitude to ensure that you're not overbearing and bossy — people will be turned off and will seek to avoid you.

Be Fanatical About Loving and Forgiveness

Nearly everyone has been hurt by the actions or words of another from childhood to adulthood. Perhaps your spouse criticized your parenting skills, your colleague sabotaged a project, or your partner had an affair. These wounds can leave you with lasting feelings of anger, bitterness, or even vengeance.

But if you don't practice forgiveness, you might be the one who pays most dearly. By embracing forgiveness, you can also embrace peace, hope, gratitude, and joy. Consider how forgiveness can lead you down the path of physical, emotional, and spiritual well-being.

He who loves his brother abides in the light, and there is no cause for stumbling in him.
(1 John 2:10).

Christians will avoid a lot of problems if they will just commit themselves to an unconditional love for their brethren. The practice of loving the brethren — all the brethren, not just the lovable ones — keeps us from stumbling. Never forget that Jesus takes personally how we entreat our Christian brothers and sisters. When we love even the "least" of our brethren, Jesus accepts that love toward Himself (Matt. 25:40). You cannot love the Lord any more than you love the least in the body of Christ.

"If someone says, I love God, and hates his brother, he is a liar; for he who does not love his brother whom he has seen, how can he love God whom he has not seen?" (1 John 4:20).

Be quick to forgive and don't hold grudges. Unforgiveness and bitterness is one of the greatest reasons why people get hurt in the church and is probably the greatest cause of apostasy - falling away.

Remember that unforgiveness is one of your greatest enemies. If you refuse to forgive, it will prevent God's forgiveness of your sins and could keep you out of Heaven. "For if you forgive men their trespasses, your heavenly Father will also forgive you. But if you do not forgive men their trespasses, neither will your Father forgive your trespasses." (Matt. 6:14-15).

FOUR:

Couples Leading Together While Bleeding

Everyone wants to fulfill their vision or assignment without any major pains or tragedies, but unfortunately, it just doesn't happen like that for 98% of the people we have met and know who are doing anything meaningful for God. Most people have heard the statement that success will cost you something; but when you're in ministry, we know personally that when God calls you, there are enemies to your assignment.

A cycle that many married couples fall into when a hurt occurs in their marriage is to clam up about the issue, withdraw from one another, dwell too much on the hurt, hold onto a grudge, walk on eggshells around one another, dig in their heels on the issue, allow bitterness to build, and end up in a cold war and deep disillusionment.

Challenges Every Couple May Face

- Overstepping or Lack of Boundaries...
- Lacking Complete Communication...
- Declining Occurrences of Sexual Intimacy...
- Wandering Focuses...
- Emotional Infidelity...
- Fighting About Money...
- Waning Appreciation and Respect ...
- Technology Interference ... Social Media
- Selfishness
- Distrust Caused by Insecurity
- Different Views on How to Handle Children or Employees
- Losing Control of Temper
- Changing Future Ambitions

Every marriage experiences problems. No matter how long you have been married – whether four years or 40 years – you will have problems. Marital problems can be extremely intense and painful, and those hurts can cut deeply and last a very long time.

The pain caused by someone you care about as much as your spouse may be very difficult to deal with, especially in ministry. Most of us have preconceived ideas about how our spouses should treat us, while at the same time we know scripturally how we should treat each other. We expect mistreatment from other people, but not from our spouses who are serving God. Just remember that as human beings, we often think, feel, and behave in ways that are hurtful, even toward those we love. Flawed people, although saved, can treat each other in flawed ways; so, no matter how much we care, we'll sometimes hurt each other.

> *Your marriage isn't doomed because you hurt or offend one another at times, have difficulty communicating, or have disagreements over little or important issues.*
> *Your marriage, ministry or business will be doomed when you don't know how to humble yourself and factor God into the equation and get help.*

We have found over the years that no relationship comes with a lifetime problem-free guarantee, because things happen, called *life*; this is in addition to a spiritual enemy that rises against one's marriage and ministry. Even men and women who grew up in stable homes, who attend church and consider themselves Christians, who promise each other "until death do us part", can have it all fall apart in the blink of an eye.

I recently received the shocking news that a dear brother in our organization passed within eight months after finding out he had cancer. What a shock to his wife and congregation. Another ministry couple found themselves entrapped in a sexual masquerade that tore their family and church in half. This was the result of one of them opening a door to spiritual seduction and manipulation, because they were bleeding (not meeting each other's needs) and didn't know how to humble themselves and ask for help.

As Christians, we know that applying biblical principles to marriage will give us a stronger foundation, unlike that of our unbelieving friends and neighbors. We know this, but what are we doing about it? In other words, what makes a marriage "Christian"?

According to author, Gary Thomas, we're not asking the right questions. What if your relationship isn't as much about you and your spouse as it is about you and God?

Instead of asking why we have struggles in the first place, the more important issue is *how we deal with them*. And, if we don't learn how to handle the pains of being bruised, cut, and sometimes feeling beat up, we will just bleed to death in the silence of our own pain. Why? Because we choose to place a bandage on the wound and not address the wound by getting surgery. Why? Because most of us are afraid to let people know that we are bleeding; so, we die in silence.

The purpose of this book is to assist people and couples leading in ministry, business, or family life in learning and receiving wisdom on how to handle the pains or challenges they will face. We want them to learn how to stop the bleeding that sometimes takes place in marriage, ministry, family, and business as a result of the storms of life; or, learn to handle problems associated with just plain old personality conflicts and offenses that will occur.

Couples have been experiencing and solving problems on their own since the beginning of time. We see the conflict between Adam and Eve, and the same kinds of issues continue to this very day. However, the more experience and maturity a couple develops in a marriage, the more success will be gained in managing and solving problems. God created us with the ability to successfully manage relationships in a healthy and productive way, whether in marriage, family, or ministry.

According to recent data from the Bureau of Labor Statistics, approximately 1.4 million businesses in the U.S. are run by a husband-and-wife team. With this number steadily rising, it's clear that modern couples are finding ways to work with their spouse and have an incredibly fulfilling career and marriage. But how?

Life is filled with a variety of wonderful blessings that God has given us to enjoy. But it is true, too, if we look realistically at the other side of the coin, life is also much like a jungle. It is a sinful and fallen world that operates under the dominating, sinister, and deceptive policies of one whom the Bible describes as "the ruler of this world" and "the God of this age" (2 Cor. 4:4).

Because of Satan's deceitful activities and the devastating effects of the fall of man (as recorded in Genesis 3), which includes a creation that groans under the curse enacted because of the fall, we live in a cruel world that is often extremely hostile.

For nearly two centuries, Beethoven's death was a mystery. The famous musician suffered from irritability, depression, and abdominal pain. His dying wish was that his illness would be discovered so that "the world may be reconciled to me after my death".

In 1994, two Americans launched a study to determine the cause of Beethoven's end. Chemical analysis of a strand of his hair showed his killer—lead poisoning. More than likely, it was a little poison in everyday activities that took his life.

It could have come from drinking out of lead-lined cups or having dinner on a lead-lined plate—both common household items in that day. Or, perhaps, it came from eating contaminated fish or even the extensive consumption of wine. It didn't come all at once; but, instead, the lead killed him slowly and quietly—one little bit of poison at a time.

That's also how hurtful bitterness destroys a marriage or organization. It stores itself in the soul, and slowly poisons the one who carries it. It's a blade meant for another that eventually severs the hand that tightly conceals it.

The effectiveness of your labors and efforts together will never rise above your ability to lead and influence others. You cannot consistently produce on a level higher than your level of leadership. But often, we are so concerned about the "product" of leadership that we sidestep the process. There are no shortcuts to leadership. No slick technique or the hottest methodology learned from the most recent seminar will cover up for a lack of character or competency.

- Never bleed down, bleed up! Before Jesus went to the cross, He didn't share His pain and misery with the disciples, He cried out to God. Don't allow pride to prevent you from going to a counselor or coach!

- Choose to love each other, even in those moments when you struggle to like each other. Love is a commitment, not a feeling.

- Embrace vulnerability and feelings, even if they are uncomfortable. It's the only way you'll ever understand your spouse. It's the only way you'll understand yourselves.

- Let go of anger. Embrace love boldly. Practice forgiveness. And when you hurt your lover's feelings, set your pride aside, take her in your arms and say, "I'm sorry." Sometimes even if you know you're right. It heals the deepest wounds.

- In every argument, remember that there won't be a "winner" and a "loser." You are partners in everything, so you'll either win together or lose together. Work together to find a solution.

> *"Be men who fight against the ripples and currents that hold back love. Who fight against the darkest shadows. Who create blueprints and music that flow from unrestrained hearts and end up touching the lives of those who know you. Especially your wives."*
> By Doug and Leslie Gustafson

FIVE:

Take Off the Mask

The webster dictionary defines a masquerade as "a party, dance, or other festive gathering of persons Wearing masks and other disguises, and often elegant, historical, or fantastic costumes."

If we truly want the character of Christ, we must expose our weaknesses, shed our hypocrisy and stop pretending. God calls us to BE TRANSPARENT.

We have met so many leaders who put on a good show and pretend to be something that they are not. Maybe you, like my wife and me, know what it's like to pretend and put on a good stage show on Sundays when you walk through the church doors after having intense, heated, and intriguing words expressed to each other.

We have watched people in music departments, deacons' boards, and even pastoral staffs who do not like each other, and in some cases can't stand the sight of a co-worker or volunteer, but act like they are cool with each other.

I know pastors who don't like other pastors because of their denominational affiliation. We have spoken to leaders who don't even like the members they Shepherd—and vice versa, all because of an offense or personality conflict. This, my friends, is sad.

I read where Pastor Paul Tan wrote, "We greet our customers professionally because we want to get the deal. We prioritize leadership over servanthood, so we are more concerned about looking elegant and demonstrating our authority than being a blessing to others."

If God has called you to an office of Shepherd, you should smell like sheep and not do ministry alone.

Pastors are notorious for their lone ranger approach to ministry. It's what I call the number one failure of 90 percent of pastors. They prefer to go it alone because of their experiences with people.

Even Jesus needed a buddy. "He came to the disciples and found them sleeping, and said to Peter, 'So, you men could not keep watch with me for one hour?'" (Matthew 26:40)
Sometimes it helps to have someone nearby, praying, loving, caring, even hurting with you. At some point, it's time to take off the mask that the real you hides behind, so that the Holy Spirit can heal you and clean you up; then, you can show your family and your neighbors who Jesus Christ really is!

Some people become involved in certain types of ministry only as a steppingstone to their ultimate goal. We use, misuse, and abuse people for our own gain. We want to go up, but we don't ever want to come down—to humble ourselves. We chase increase, abundance, glamour, success, and name and fame so that we look good on the outside at the expense of our inward man; yet, we are really hurting and bleeding on the inside while we smile and work on our Golden Globe awards. There are so many people who pretend to be something that they are not.

Do you ever feel like you are wearing a mask? Do you ever find yourself pretending to be someone you're not? Pretending to "have it all together", but in reality, your "all together" is falling apart? You would never want people to see the "real you", the person behind the mask. You would be embarrassed if you were ever "found out".

So...we put on our masks, go about our business, and when friends ask how we are, we smile and declare, "Blessed and highly favored!" Get Real... How are you *really* doing?

Because so many of us are wearing these perfection masks, we look around and think that we are the only Christian mom or father or pastor who is "messing up". We feel like failures. We would never admit to needing help, let alone actually *asking* for it! That's Pride, my friend!

I have watched so many people and leaders in the Body of Christ, who, instead of building one another up and encouraging each other in our faith, we pretend that we are just fine and hide behind our masks of hurt and pain. The root of a lot of this is *pride*.

The Bible says "pride goeth before the fall," Proverbs 16:18. In spite of this known scripture, people in the western culture are among the proudest people in the world.

> *Who are you sharing the deep spiritual stuff of your life with?*
> *Who is mentoring you, spiritually (and who are you mentoring)? Are you trying to do the Christian life all on your own?*

I read an article where one minister said, "I know a lot about 'pride' and its religious counterpart, 'self-righteousness'. There was a time where I would classify myself as an expert in both arenas, not from studying the subjects, but from actually wearing those fashionable garments for a period of time." He stated, "That's why I can spot that spirit out a mile away. Every now and then when it tries to jump on me or the mask looks appealing, I have to rebuke it. You see, pride and self-righteousness run deep."

To me "pride" is different from "self-righteous". I see pride as something worldly, whereas self-righteousness is a religious spirit that tends to focus on one's position between God and man.

I see leaders like this all the time, and it's a turn off. There are a lot of leaders who can wear both garments, pride and self-righteousness. If I had to describe what these garments looked like, I would probably describe them as hats, robes, or dresses to be worn backwards where the back of the hood on the robe actually covered one's face.

I say this because both pride and self-righteousness blind our ability to see things as they really are. The worst part of this blindness is that the blind person does not believe they are blind. To others, it is obvious, but to the poor souls wearing the garments of pride and self-righteousness, they actually believe they see. And they always see themselves in a different light than others see them.

But God sees through the mask right down to the "real you". He sees all the flaws and mistakes and failures and, yet, loves us completely and unconditionally. Isn't it comforting to know how much He loves us?

Psalm 139 tells us that God searches us and knows us. He knows us completely, from the inside out. He knows a word before it even reaches our tongue. He is familiar with our ways. He isn't surprised by us. He knows every thought, every worry, every joy, every hurt and pain. Even when we cover up our wounds, He sees the need for healing.

There is no where we can run from His Spirit, nowhere to escape His love, no mask to hide our person from Him. With God, we can stop pretending, take off our mask, and allow Him to love us.

But the Lord made it clear that the outside is not what matters to Him when He told Samuel: "'Do not look at his appearance or at his physical stature, because I have refused him. For the Lord does not see as man sees; for man looks at the outward appearance, but the Lord looks at the heart'" (1 Sam.16:7, NKJV). Samuel was in the process of determining which son of Jesse God wanted to become king of Israel, and Samuel was tempted to use criteria other than God's to make the choice.

The Bible tells us that when Solomon built the temple, he laid the foundation with "large stones, costly stones, and hewn stones" (1 King 5:17). Apparently, he wanted the foundation to be the best, even though no one would see it.

If we were builders, we would be more likely to use regular stones to construct the foundation, as long as it was strong. We probably would not spend extra money on costly stones for something that would not be seen. But Solomon was different. The foundation was important to him. It is just as important to God. God is building a spiritual house, and we are the spiritual stones He is building it with.

He puts a lot of emphasis on the heart and the mind, which are invisible to the natural eyes. Why? Because when they are renewed, these invisible things will transform our attitudes, habits and character, and lead us into our destiny. He is preparing us from the inside out. That's why we need the Helper, the Holy Spirit, to assist us in doing that which we find so hard to do by ourselves.

While paracletos does always refer to the Lord in those scriptures, the word parakleesis (also a noun), for comfort or consolation, may refer both to the work of the Lord in our lives as well as the effect we have upon each other.

Don't miss that.
Here, the Apostle Paul said:

We were afflicted on every side, conflicts without, fears within. But God, who comforts the humble, comforted us by the coming of Titus. And, not only by his coming, but also by the comfort with which he was comforted in you, as he reported to us your longing, your mourning, your zeal for me; so that I rejoiced even more. (II Corinthians 7:5-7).

The great apostle was hurting. He needed something, which God provided by way of a friend, Titus. When this messenger reported to Paul how faithfully the Corinthians were serving God, when he told how they cared for Paul and grieved over him, that pumped him up.

Titus himself was elated by the work of the Corinthians, Paul says.

God made us to need the companionship of fellow disciples. Don't allow the enemy to get into your head and tell you that you don't need anyone! God made us gregarious. We are social creatures. We do not do well in isolation. We are all about "social networking", to use a term on everyone's tongues today.

Now is the time to take off your mask, because God wants to develop your character and shape you to fulfill your God-ordained destiny. It's not something you can do on your own; it is the work of the Holy Spirit in you. But you can cooperate with God by putting yourself in a position to be transformed. Don't be a statistic pulpit hypocrite!

Ask yourself these questions:

- Do I have someone I'm accountable to other than God?

- Do I have someone who can speak into my life? Can I be totally honest and transparent with this person, and can I accept correction with an open heart and mind?

- When someone hurts me, do I forgive them and allow God to avenge me? Or, do I become bitter and retaliate?

- When I forgive someone who has wronged me, do I release him and continue to love him as before, or put him on a probation period?

- Do I rejoice in my "enemy's" tragedy?

- Men: Do I look at women with lust or fantasy in my heart?

- Women: Do I dress to entice men with my physical appearance?

- Do I use my outward appearance or intelligence as a "cover" or "mask" because of insecurity?

If your answers let you know your heart is not in the condition God wants it to be, go to Him now, just as you are. You don't need to hide behind a mask. He is interested in you. He loves you and wants to set you free from any condemnation—and from the bondage of your sin.

Remember, Jesus came to seek not the righteous, but sinners! He said it is not the healthy who need a physician, but the sick. His grace is sufficient for you. As God completes His work in you, you will begin to reflect not a false image of yourself, but the character of His Son Jesus Christ. Let Him be Lord and Savior of your life!

SIX:

Maintain Your Position with God

I believe that there are times in the life of every Believer, even though you are walking by faith and there is no known sin in your life, God seems far away. You pray, but God doesn't answer. You read the Bible, but He does not speak to you. You seek God, but it seems as if He is hiding. You wanted God to deal with a matter or do something for you and it just doesn't happen.

What do a lot of people do? They move away from God and allow the enemy to speak and lie to them about what God isn't, or how there is no hope nor even help for their situation. Then they give in to their emotions, which leads to you making all the flesh decisions. Let's look at Jeremiah.

> *"For My people have committed two*
> *evils: They have forsaken Me,*
> *The fountain of living waters,*
> *To hew for themselves cisterns, roken*
> *cisterns That can hold no water."*
> *Jeremiah 2:13 (NASB)*

God's people committed two evils. One, they had forsaken... abandoned...God. The other, they had dug their own cisterns.

To understand the full impact of this scripture, you must look a little closer at the historical context. Jeremiah preached and lived in a day when the people of Judah, the southern portion of the nation of Israel, had turned away from the Living God to do their own thing. And God, through Jeremiah, compared this to digging for themselves cisterns. A cistern was an artificial reservoir that was dug in the earth or hewn in the rock for the collection and storage of water...rainwater, runoff water, etc.

Cisterns were very important in the land of Israel because of the long, dry season, and the few natural springs. Rainfall was scarce during the summer months, and it was important that water be stored during the rainy months for the upcoming dry season. But a broken cistern was practically worthless!

A broken or cracked cistern could possibly hold a small quantity of dirty water, but very little, if any! And notice that the cisterns did not become broken after some time of holding water...NO...*they were broken from the day they were built*...they never held any water!

Maybe we could try to excuse them for digging their own cisterns. Maybe they were just going through a tough time and had been through some stressful situations and they just wanted to be sure their bases were covered. But that was only HALF of what they did wrong! Trying to construct an artificial reservoir for collecting spiritual water was bad enough, but to turn away and reject the water from the life-giving spring was tragic!

If we find ourselves bleeding and leaking or gushing hurt because of offenses or life just not going the way we want it to, ask yourself this question: "Have we foolishly gotten involved in constructing our own cisterns?" Wealth, fame, recognition, honor, position, power, and pleasure...friends, props, traditions, merits...anything trusted besides God...they are cisterns at best, whose water will putrefy...or broken vessels, which will leave you nothing but mud and dirt at the end. Sometimes we bleed because things aren't working out the way we envision it, or the warfare that we face pushes us away from God.

Sometimes, some of us try to bring fulfillment to our lives by things and stuff or building ourselves up to be something that we really aren't because of a spiritual void. Any of these things are not wrong in themselves, and they can be good and helpful when kept in proper balance. But when we find that we are _looking to these things_ for satisfaction and fulfillment in life or ministry, a subtle form of cistern deconstruction is probably going on.

You and I know better, but we do it anyway. We involve ourselves with every project that comes down the pike trying to fill the void that only Christ can fill. Understand WHO your Source is and the position He has placed you in to be a vessel of honor and carrier of His kingdom message.

The three things that cisterns were used for:

- Provision
- Prison
- Graves

When we have misdirected worship (addictions to drugs, alcohol, pornography, shopping, internet, sports, outward appearance, personal agenda, etc.) …at first, they seem to satisfy – PROVISION. Then, you find it is your – PRISON. Finally, it will be your – GRAVE.

God gave the nation of Judah chance after chance to return to the Lord, but they turned further and further away. I've watched people over the years who God showed grace and mercy, which was so evident, and you thought they would have turned from the way that they thought was right, but the enemy blinded them in such a way that it seared their conscience.

God wants you to get your eyes off of the well that has been dug by men who have hurt you, or manipulated you, and get your eyes upon the Living Water that comes only from Him. As long as you go to an empty well (human beings and material things), you will leave with disappointment and discouragement. But every time you come to the Lord, you will leave the old water buckets and go get refreshed with a drink of Living Water.

John 7:37-38 – "In the last day, that great day of the feast, Jesus stood and cried, saying, If any man thirst, let him come unto me, and drink. He that believeth on me, as the scripture hath said, out of his belly shall flow rivers of living water." This was a picture of the people of Israel.

They laughed at Jeremiah's metaphor, but in reality, they were laughing at themselves, because they had rejected the true God who was called *"the spring of living water"*. Instead, they were relying on their own efforts to satisfy the longings of their souls and their urgent need of water.

They had strayed from God whom the psalmist called *"the fountain of life"*, and they went after other gods. (Psalm 36:9) Don't fall prey to changing the Gospel so that the majority will accept you and cheer for you.

> *Don't desire the popularity and cheers of men, because everyone who cheers you will eventually boo you!*
> *- Anthony McFarland*

They had tried to find satisfaction in various sins and other futile attempts to fill their lives. How many people do we see in church like that? But their attempts were like trying to fill broken cisterns. Whatever they were able to accumulate became stagnant, and they were unable to hold onto much of what they could find.

They were trying to accumulate things, but they had nothing of real value.

There was a stench in their nostrils, and their lives were empty because they were unwilling to turn to the true God Who could give them real life, which was lasting and fulfilling.

They did not trust the Lord to satisfy their thirst.

Jeremiah said: *We all are thirsty.* In other words, he was saying that there are thirsts and longings in our lives that are placed there by God.

We need for our lives to have real meaning. We are searching for a lasting purpose in which we can invest our lives.

We are looking for love and intimacy.

We want joy and happiness.

We want peace.

We want freedom.

All of these longings are a part of what all of us have.

We are created in the likeness of God, and these are the things that He wants us to have. He has created us to have these hungers and thirsts, and the question is:

How can these longings and hungers be fulfilled in our lives?

It is not a sin to be thirsty, but satisfying that thirst in selfish ways can be sinful.

It is not a sin to desire love, but how we decide to meet our need for love can be sinful.

It is not a sin for us to want meaning and purpose in our lives, but if our life's primary purpose and meaning is not within God's will for us, then it is sinful.

It is not a sin to desire freedom, unless we desire to be free from God, then it is sinful.

It is not a sin for us to seek happiness, but when we seek happiness outside the will of God, it is sinful.

SEVEN:

Team Conflicts Can Cause Bleeding

There are many areas of a church and business where conflict can develop. However, most of them tend to fall under one of three categories: *conflict due to blatant error among Believers*; *conflict with leadership*; *conflict between those working in ministry*. Admittedly, many issues can cross over and actually involve two or more of these categories.

The small church revolves around the close relationships formed within the congregation. Because of this, many believe that a small church is a place where deeply caring people who love one another and mutually support each other gather to worship, where conflicts are nonexistent, and where "never is heard a discouraging word." While this is true of *some* smaller congregations, it is not true of every congregation all the time.

Being a Christian pastor today is more difficult than at any time in history. In this century, we witnessed the collapse of the Christian consensus that held American culture together for centuries. The moral relativism that accompanies a secular view of reality deeply affects the work of the church and its leadership.

There is an anti-Christ spirit in our culture and throughout media that is programming people to have a shaded view of church and its leaders like never before. Far too many good pastors and families are being driven out of ministry, leaving thousands of churches weak and vulnerable to spiritual attack. Without good Spirit-Filled leadership, denominational factions multiply, evangelism declines, divorces proceed unrestrained, discipleship loses direction, and ministries who evangelize are forgotten.

Membership conflict, defined as *a difference in opinion or purpose that frustrates someone's goals or desires*, may occur when those religious and spiritual beliefs are unaligned. We find so many levels of power struggle taking place, which I view, along with spiritual warfare; and my wife likes to say, "People are being used willingly or unwillingly by the devil."

Remember, we set the example for our team to follow in how you and I handle conflict. We can be used by God or used by the enemy.

Conflict is a reality that confronts people attending your ministry, regardless of how loving and caring the people are. The difference between a loving flock and one settling into patterns of warfare is not the amount of conflict or the intensity of conflict, but *the way they respond to and resolve conflict*. Conflict of some form or fashion is an inevitable occurrence in a relationship.

A team of Brigham Young University researchers have studied how couples can manage conflict when their personality styles are mismatched. And, some of your team members will not like how you handle conflict, but there is a grace on you as a pastor to handle the problems of personality conflict.

Having the right understanding of the definition of team conflict and being able to classify all conflicts between employees and volunteers into types will allow team leaders and managers to look into the actual reasons of group conflicts and find solutions that help resolve interpersonal problems. Although conflicts are inevitable, decision-makers should strive to reduce the likelihood of conflict occurrence.

Every leader who is partnering in marriage or business must understand that you cannot allow outside conflict to cause the two of you to open the door to it and permit it to enter into your marriage or partnership.

Sometimes a pastor is forced out of ministry due to failure to resolve differences with other people within the church. Conflict is not necessarily bad. The Bible, the collection of sacred writings of the Christian faith, teaches that some differences are natural and beneficial. Christians believe that God created people as unique individuals, with different opinions, convictions, desires, perspectives, and priorities.

Never forget, when conflict is handled righteously, disagreements in the church in these areas can stimulate productive dialogue, encourage creativity, and promote helpful change and growth.

Every leader must mitigate the negative impact of group conflicts and try to increase the constructive impact of those conflicts. One of the things that every leader has to watch out for are those who bleed on the other team members and congregation. People who bleed have the potential to become toxic, because they are hurt and don't understand there is a right and wrong way to bleed.

As a quick sidebar, leaders must teach the leaders under them not to privately listen to members or volunteers who are hemorrhaging and who really need *your* attention as the senior leader. Remember, conflict can change your environment. And the wrong environment will cultivate the wrong spirit of criticism, causing chaos and confusion, because persons may be acting out of hurt. All of this is subtly designed to steal, kill, and destroy your ministry or business.

Team Conflict is an interpersonal problem that occurs between two or more members of a team, and affects results of teamwork, so the team does not perform at optimum levels. Team conflicts are caused by the situation when the balance between perceptions, goals, or/and values of the team are upset; therefore, people can no longer work together, and no shared goals can be achieved in the team environment.

According to Professors Dean Busby and Thomas Holman, different perspectives do not necessarily doom relationship quality.

Information was accumulated from nearly 2,000 couples with the results published in a recent issue of the academic journal, *Family Process*.

> *"The concern with mismatched couples is that they will have problems that are just never quite resolvable,"* Holman said.

> *"The concern with personality conflict amongst volunteers is that their problems will bleed over into their departments, causing extreme difficulty,"* says Dr. McFarland.

> *"But it's really about getting to a point where a problem becomes less important to them than the relationship itself, and for volunteers to understand that getting to a place where problems don't affect the work of God is more important." We must all remove 'self from the work of God!"*

So, what are the conflict styles, and which one fits your personality? And how can you work through a mismatched personality pairing in your department or team?

The "Avoidant"

Avoidant people minimize conflict as much as possible. They still interact with their spouse or co-workers but avoid contentious issues. They think there is little to gain from getting openly angry, and that problems have a way of working themselves out if you just relax, let go, and trust God.

The "Endorser"

Validating people make certain that both sides are heard and that their partner's views are appreciated. They believe in remaining calm and displaying self-control. These individuals are led by the Holy Spirit. They spend equal amounts of time validating others and searching for a compromise.

The "Volatile"

Volatile people are usually more passionate, louder and more energetic; they don't shy away from a lively debate. They believe that differences are resolved by getting everything out in the open. Their intensity is often balanced with kind and loving expressions. Sometimes they are viewed in a wrong light and bring judgmental views upon themselves because of their tact or expression, which can be viewed as aggressive.

The "Antagonistic"

The only non-functional style, hostile people can be described as destructive. In conflict, they try to tear the other person down and, at times, stonewall all contact with their relationships. "It's hard to recover from a hostile conflict without some help, I believe," Professor Busby said. "Hostility gets to a place where you scar people." Hostility is always the cousin to the spirit, Antagonism. The ungodly love to fight and hurt people.

The worst functional mismatched conflict style is the avoidant volatile pair. The good news is that it was the least common pairing in the study, representing a little more than 1 in 10 couples.

Many people in this situation fall into the trap of attributing their co-workers or partner's motives incorrectly. Sincere attempts to resolve a conflict and restore harmony can be construed as nagging if you're walking in the flesh and not in the Spirit.

The researcher who pioneered these conflict styles, John Gottman, found that in a healthy conflict style, there are five positive exchanges for every one negative exchange. In dysfunctional styles, the negative exchanges outnumber the positive.

If you're in the middle of a conflict with other Christians, however, you might not like this passage very much. Your gut instinct is to win the battle, to be vindicated, to prevail over your opponents. But this text speaks of being agreeable, humble, and considering others as better than yourself. If you're like me when I'm duking it out with my brothers and sisters in Christ, this is not what you want to hear.

You'd probably prefer that I had sent you to Psalm 58:8, in which David prayed about his enemies: "Let them be like the snail that dissolves into slime." But, like it or not, if you're a follower of Christ, you've got to deal with Philippians 2:1-11. More to the point, you're stuck with the compelling and challenging example of Jesus Himself.

Philippians 2 begins with a series of ethical injunctions that could be paraphrased: agree with each other; love each other; be humble; care more for the concerns of others than for your own concerns. These imperatives are summarized in verse five: "Let the same mind be in you that was in Christ Jesus." In a nutshell, we are to think as Jesus thought.

Paul doesn't leave it up to us to decide what it means to think like Jesus. We don't get to pick and choose from the gospel stories or to make up our own version of what constitutes the mind of Christ. Rather, Paul shows us quite clearly in verses 6-8 what it means to think like Jesus:

Unfortunately, difficult people — whether they are members in the church, co-workers, leaders, bosses, or family — face us constantly. The way we handle them can affect our assignment, our environment, our advancement, and even our health.

Sometimes it is hard to know which principle to follow, whether to bring something up or to remain silent. These questions will help you decide:

- What are my motives?
- Is this really my problem? What is my part in it? Did I help set it up?
- Have I been loving and respectful?
- How important is this topic?
- How important is this issue to God?
- Have I been a nag?
- Should I give grace a chance?

97

Here are tips to dealing with troubled people.

- Pray and ask God for wisdom in dealing with them.
- Try not to take things personally.
- Ask questions rather than make statements.
- If you are a leader, have supporting evidence in writing.
- Ensure understanding and communication.
- Use appropriate phrases when needed.
- Separate the issue from the person.
- Express appreciation when appropriate.

At the end of the day, even if someone has a difficult personality, that person can help you learn a skill or give you insight into being a better leader. God has graced you to handle conflict and be a benefit to your church or business and those you love!

EIGHT:

When Bleeding, Manage Your Emotions

Leaders' emotions are their heart work that reflects what they feel. Many of us wrestle with our emotions and don't know if we are right or wrong for some of the emotions that we feel.

> *For our struggle is not against flesh and blood, but against the rulers, against the authorities, against the powers of this dark world and against the spiritual forces of evil in the heavenly realms. Eph. 6:12*

In the world we live in today, negative emotions have become a sign of weakness and inadequacy, forcing us to internalize how we're really feeling and creating even bigger problems often times. Because we are all human beings, however, we can't help but experience these negative feelings from time to time, causing the massive happy walls we build to come crashing down, although we know that the joy of our Lord is our strength. And while these negative feelings might make us want to crawl under a rock and declare our hatred for the universe, they're actually more beneficial than you think. For example: Sadness makes you pay attention to detail; or anxiety, on the other hand, turns you into a problem-solver as a leader. When you're anxious, you'll do anything you can to get yourself and others out of a pressing situation.

From a scientific (rather than a popular) standpoint, emotional intelligence is the ability to accurately perceive your own and others' emotions; to understand the signals that emotions send about relationships; and to manage your own and others' emotions. It doesn't necessarily include the qualities (like optimism, initiative, and self-confidence) that some popular definitions ascribe to it.

It took almost a decade after the term was coined for Rutgers psychologist, Daniel Goleman, to establish the importance of emotional intelligence to business leadership, which I believe applies to ministry as well.

Scripture has much to say also about negative emotions, beginning in Genesis when Adam and Eve experienced shame due to their sin. In Genesis 3:10, Adam experienced an unhealthy fear that caused him to hide from God. Cain expressed extreme anger toward God in Genesis 4:5,6. On many occasions, Jesus expressed His emotions. For example, He was deeply moved and wept at Lazarus' grave; He became angry with His disciples; and He had compassion for certain people such as lepers and the blind. The expression of emotions is found throughout the New Testament and concludes in Revelation where John, describing the New Jerusalem, writes, "He will wipe every tear from their eyes. There will be no more death or mourning or crying or pain, for the old order of things has passed away" (Revelation 21:4).

A leader's emotions affect his mood and the atmosphere of their home life and church. Research as well as ministry experience shows a leader's mood is contagious, spreading quickly throughout a ministry.

A good mood characterized by optimism and inspiration affects people positively. However, a bad mood characterized by negativity and pessimism will cripple a ministry and damage people.

A leader's mood has the potential to set the mood for the entire church or business. Many people have experienced or know of senior pastors or a boss who has attempted to lead using fear. In these situations, people do not follow because they want to, but because they fear the wrath of the leader. To the other extreme, your mood can have grave effects on your team and the culture of your work place.

It's interesting how quickly your mood can change, how deep your heart can sink, and how one person can really affect you. In turn, if you don't have a healthy response, you can sink the day, a person, or ship.

One male writer once said, "Women are not moody." They just have days when they can put up with more stuff and days when they are less likely to put up with your mess. Sometimes there isn't any patience left over in her cup for anyone. So, just figure out what game changers will cheer her up.

The key emotion questions for leaders are:

What emotions are liabilities for your ministry? Or, what emotions must you deal with to create a better climate for ministry or business? Everyone has emotions. Some emotions are easier to deal with, such as joy or happiness. Some emotions are harder, such as fear, anger, or sadness.

Whether you're dealing with anger, depression, or frustration, it is important to have good skills to address any emotions causing you or others distress, both in the short term and long term.

To develop emotional well-being and establish a spiritually healthy climate for ministry or marriage, leaders must cultivate two primary areas: their emotions and the emotions of the people they minister with and to.

One therapist reported that identifying a specific emotion can be more difficult than you think. If you are struggling, start with the four basic categories: anxiety, sadness, anger, or happiness. By simply identifying exactly what you're feeling, you can begin taking the power away from the emotion as you work through what's causing it.

Please understand that we all are responsible for our lives. Not only our physical lives, but for what is going on inside of us. So, ask yourself, "What is going on inside?" The Word of God says that we are to "Cast down imaginations, and every high thing that exalteth itself against the knowledge of God, and bringing into captivity every thought to the obedience of Christ."

Though your feelings (thoughts) may vary in intensity, most fall into one of these broad categories.

Anxiety often takes the shape of "what if" questions. What if they don't like me? What if I'm not accepted? Etc.
Unhappiness tends to happen when we focus on things we cannot change, such as death or loss.

Anger is the response after being attacked, such as our values.

Gladness is positive thought often around a gain, such as a compliment from a friend or a reward, like a promotion at work.

The first area relates to the leaders' emotions and is twofold.

<u>Capacity 1</u>: Leaders must understand and manage their own emotions. Understanding their emotions involves taking four steps:

- Step 1: Leaders must learn to recognize their emotions when they occur.

- Step 2: Leaders should identify their emotions. Look for: anger, anxiety, sadness, fear, shame, discouragement, surprise, joy, and love.

- Step 3: Leaders must deal biblically with the destructive emotions. For example, Ephesians 4:26 addresses sinful anger, and Philippians 4:6,7 addresses worry and anxiety.

- Step 4: Leaders may want to explore why they are experiencing certain emotions.

"'For I know the thoughts that I think toward you, says the Lord, thoughts of peace and not of evil, to give you a future and a hope'" (Jer. 29:11, NKJV). God's thoughts are of abundance and not lack.

He wants you to live large and to bring you into a good life. Toward this end, He gives you divine inspirational thoughts and the ability to speak them into existence so that you will grow to fulfill His best plan for your life.

He wants you to mature in wisdom, authority, and supernatural ability so that you can bear witness to the splendor of His kingdom. Your miracle is already in existence, but it is up to you to learn to see it and to call it out.

In Matthew 21:2, when Jesus was preparing for His final entry into Jerusalem, He called for a donkey to be brought to Him, but the donkey stayed tied up until Jesus called for it. Likewise, the thing you need might already be waiting for you, but you don't see it yet because *you haven't called for it*. A situation or circumstance generally comes because you have called it to yourself—you have given it permission to exist in your life.

Once leaders begin to understand their emotions. Next, they must manage their emotions. To accomplish this, they need to remember two things:

1. They cannot control being swept by their emotions because the emotional mind often overrides the rational mind, such as when a person loses his temper.

2. They can, however, control how they respond to or handle their emotions. They can recognize them and deal biblically with them in the power of the Holy Spirit.

Capacity 2: Leaders must not only be aware of and work on their own emotions, but also recognize others' emotions and help them manage them as well.

This is commonly referred to as empathy. Most people have been in situations where an emotionally unhealthy person, whether in a leadership position or not, negatively affects a ministry. It is imperative that leaders deal with these people for the sake of the ministry and to help the individual. How do leaders accomplish this? Much the same way they handle their own emotions, only they apply the four steps above to the individual who needs help.

In a post written by Julie Bassett several years ago, she shared that, "Capacity is defined as 'the maximum amount that something (or someone) can contain.'" She went on to say how she was at a conference and Dr. Sam Chand (whom I think very highly of) was speaking and "he delivered some absolute gold when it comes to pastoring and leading people. Something he said that resounded with me in regards to capacity was that 'you will only grow to the threshold of your pain.'"

In other words, if your threshold of pain is low, you will only grow to that level. In order to grow more, you need to allow your capacity for pain to increase. The pain he was talking about, of course, wasn't physical pain, but more emotional pain and spiritual struggle.

I always find it interesting that two people can go through the same issue but can have radically different responses to their situation. Where one person will determine in their heart that they will push through, lean in, find solutions and come out the other side stronger, another person will see it as an opportunity to make excuses, become ineffective and allow opportunity to be wasted.

Capacity is a huge indicator as to how far you will go in life. If you have any sort of vision for your life, it is going to require a big capacity to accomplish it. The encouraging thing is that capacity isn't a stagnant, unmoving outcome. It has the ability to change, enlarge, and move according to our response.

We live in a world that needs to be reached for the gospel, and that is going to take not just a group of passionate people, but a group of big capacity, whatever-it-takes people who are willing to make sacrifices for the sake of the gospel.

Capacity will always determine the outcome of the opportunities that come our way.

Regardless of how big you think your capacity is, it could always be enlarged even more.

One pastor shared his heart and said, "As I review my own 18 years of church planting, the pain of conflicts and the brokenness that it brings into my emotional life, has been *the* factor to cause me to flag and question my ability and willingness to continue leading.

A few years ago, I met with my doctor for an annual exam, and he told me that my cholesterol was out of balance again. What was interesting, he told me, "Pastor Anthony, your eating or diet isn't the problem, it's your level of stress that's affecting your health!" My initial response to him was, "Doctor, I am a man of faith and don't have any stress." He turned and said graciously to me, "Pastor, every leader has stress, and especially pastors.'"

Many of the leaders who have left ministry have often done so, overwhelmed by a tidal wave of conflict, stress, pain, and relational brokenness.

Sometimes, ministry and marriage can hurt. Sometimes that pain lasts longer than seems bearable. It is an old adage that says, "Hurt people hurt people." Those who have been emotionally damaged tend to inflict their hurt and pain on other people. For example, a large percentage of those who have been sexually abused become the abusers of others. Those who suffered under an alcoholic parent often cause their future family to suffer because of their drunken stupors. Why? They don't want to confront the strongholds in their life.

****

True Story of an Anonymous Leader
Real Life Story/Real Lessons

A prominent pastor who resigned from his church after revealing that he was guilty of a "moral failure" spoke out as he had to cope with the very public fallout, revealing the two key conclusions that he had come to in recent months regarding his sinfulness and "God's grace."

"I've been forced to face myself in a deeper way than I ever have, and I've come to two conclusions,"

Pastor Clyde told a popular podcast. "I'm far worse than I ever thought I was [and] God's grace is infinitely greater than I could have ever hoped for or imagined."

Clyde, 40, who recently vacated his position as pastor of a large church in New York, spoke out in an in-depth interview discussing his sins and the obstacles that he has faced in recent months.

"I'm alive and breathing, and I am doing far better than I deserve," Clyde said when asked how he's currently faring.

"This is the darkest season of my life. I'm 40 years old and have never experienced a season this dark before," Clyde said. "I am experiencing the weight of the law. I've lost everything — book deals cancelled, lost my job, all my speaking engagements canceled, reputation soiled — I mean everything."

The pastor was candid as he shared the struggles that he has faced, including frustrations with God and the church — and his attempt to blame someone other than himself for what unfolded — all paradigms that he said were spiritually unhealthy.

"Of course, there's no freedom in that," he said, saying that he's both "sick and sorry" for all that unfolded.

When the scandal first broke in the media, Clyde said that he was "very, very" isolated, beating himself up as he considered the weight of his actions and the impact that they would have on his children, the church, and the credibility of the gospel.

But he explained that he is now finding grace and redemption as God has surrounded him with good people who are helping him through.

Clyde, who said that he is "swimming in the sea" of his consequences, is hoping to let people see his profound brokenness, as he journeys through the recovery process.

"I can only hope and pray that, in time, as God heals me and as God reveals more of himself to me that I will — by his grace — emerge from this healthier and more humble and more excited about his amazing grace and outrageous mercy than I ever have before," he said.

Clyde said that he is thankful for God's grace and forgiveness and that he's now speaking out as he journeys through the process in an effort to "practice what I have been preaching".

While many preachers who are embroiled in scandal disappear and reemerge once they have dealt with their problems, Clyde said that he has always been open in his ministry about his struggles; now, he plans to continue doing the same, even though the process hasn't been easy.

"My sin and by badness is being broadcast through the world, seemingly on a daily basis," he said. "I feel like crawling into a hole and dying on most days."

During the podcast interview, news broke that Clyde had filed for divorce from his wife.

Clyde's personal counselor said, "Much grace, counsel, thought, prayer and action has been invested over a six-month period of time with the hope of healing the marriage, but sadly, there are times when the trust is so deeply broken and patterns so set in place that it seems best to recognize that brokenness, cry out for God's grace, mourn, commit to forgiveness, rest in the truths of the gospel and with a grieved heart, move on."

He continued, "I remain committed to Clyde as a brother and counselor and I will continue to give him the gospel as he now deals with what we together hoped and prayed would not happen."

Clyde, who said that his life has forever changed, offered a candid assessment of where things currently stand after telling a very large newspaper last year that his marriage has been in turmoil after discovering that his wife, Kim, was having an affair; he also admitted at the time that he subsequently had an affair of his own.

"My family and I are, at every imaginable level, overwhelmed. What life will look like from here on out is completely unknown to us. And that scares me," Clyde wrote, "but we are alive and not without hope. We are certain that better and brighter days are ahead."

The preacher said that he spends most of his days looking for a job in an effort to continue providing for his family, noting that a nagging question has been on his mind — one that presumably led him to post the open letter.

"One of the big questions I've wrestled with is, 'How do I properly steward this glorious ruin?' To be quite honest, I want to crawl into a hole and be anonymous for a long, long time. I don't want a stage, a platform, a microphone, a spotlight. I want to disappear," Clyde continued. "Nothing seems more appealing to me on most days than to simply vanish."

While many people want to portray only their good and positive experience and qualities, Clyde said that he would be undermining the very gospel message that he embraces if he only showed a "polished" version of himself.

Despite wanting to retreat amid the chaos, he said that he wants to be authentic.

"If I run away because I don't want you to see me broken and weak and sad and angry and struggling with fear and guilt and shame, then I fail to practice what I preach — and one of the many things I've learned from this is that failing to practice what you preach is destructive," he wrote. "The gospel frees me to let you see me at my worst — the me that runs away, the me that doesn't want to pray, the me who gets angry at God, the me who rationalizes, the me that knows I'm solely to blame for my sinful choice but who wants to blame others."

Clyde added, "That's my shadow side. And it's dark. I knew I was bad, but I never knew I was this bad."

The pastor went on to say that "grace always flows to the lowest point", admitting that he's scared to let people see him "at the bottom", but he plans to share updates as he journeys through healing. He concluded by thanking people for their prayers.

Wisdom Nuggets

Until we as leaders deal with the whole person, as shown in 1 Thessalonians 5:23, our congregations will be filled with people who are spiritually gifted but act like emotional infants and leaky cisterns. The church must deal with emotional health and not just spiritual health, faith and power.

What can you do when marriage and ministry hurts? How can you overcome the pain?
We need a biblical understanding and revelation on the power of pain, which is often a sign that there is internal bleeding in some cases.

I recommend for every leadership team to read the book Leading with a Limp and Resolving Conflict on how to be transformed by Pain and Weakness by Dr. Dan Allender. It diagnoses the pathologies of conflicts in leadership, detailing how we often abuse others, or are overwhelmed ourselves in conflict. It brings understanding and hope to see how we can face our brokenness with others and learn from it and become better leaders. In fact, our ability to face our brokenness and weakness determines what kind of leader we are.

The next powerful read is *Leading Through Pain* by Dr. Sam Chad. This book, by his own admission, is not a theology of pain, or a biblical study in pain, but is rather an exploration of leading in times of pain and brokenness. As I read it, the stories of conflicts helped me get perspective, and the leadership information within it gave me steps and actions on how to lead through conflict and pain.

NINE:

Required Surgery to Stop the Hemorrhaging

I have been told that in order to get rid of cancer, you must attack it. The same, again, is true of bitterness or a bad heart—you must attack it. I have found that asking the simple question of "Why am I bitter towards X?" is a great place to start. The answer is often something like, "…because I don't feel like they respect or honor me." Other responses are usually, "They lied to me." Or, "They didn't follow through on their promise," etc.

> *Just like cancer, bitterness grows over time unless treated.*

Have you ever seen a piece of moldy bread? It appears that there is only one ruined area, but if you were to look at the bread through a microscope, you would see long roots spreading throughout the slice. What appears on the surface doesn't reflect what's really happening beneath.

Bitterness grows the same way. One little bit of bitterness can start to spread throughout your heart and contaminate your whole body. It will start to manifest itself in your attitude, demeanor, and even your health.

In addition, the spreading can also affect your children and your family. Have you ever noticed how one person's criticism makes everyone else critical, too? It's the same with bitterness. Paul compares it to yeast when he writes, "A little leaven, leavens the whole lump" (Galatians 5:6). When you allow bitterness into your life, it extends to your family, your church body, and everyone else involved in your life.

The Bible tells us in Heb 12:15, Looking diligently lest any man fail of the grace of God; lest any root of bitterness springing up trouble *you*, and thereby many be defiled. The fruits of bitterness are anger, wrath, slander, hate, and malice (or desire to see another suffer).

You may feel like there is little hope left for your ministry or marriage relationships. You may be so full of bitterness that you've convinced yourself that your marriage or the people you work with could never be healed; but let me assure you that the healing begins with yourself. With God, all things are possible. (Matthew 19:26)

Here are the stages and symptoms of resentment:

1. Oversensitive to a verbal remark, action, or lack of action
2. Hurt feelings
3. Repulsive feeling toward a person at the thought or sight of him

4. Retaining wounds and frequently talking about them
5. Alienation of a person
6. Verbal slander against the person
7. Lack of obedience (ref Mt 5:44,45)
8. Becoming like the one you despise

Christians in the early church experienced miracles of healing as well. In fact, health and prosperity were objects of prayer for the Believers: "Beloved, I pray that you may prosper in all things and be in health, just as your soul prospers," the apostle John wrote in 3 John 1:2.

When we look at the healing ministry of Jesus, we must also recognize the vital connection we have with it: We are His body on earth today (1 Cor. 3:16). Therefore, we must exhibit the same passion for healing that we have observed in Him.

Any examination of Jesus' healing miracles during His generation will reveal facts about how He healed and whom He healed. Note that the Bible shows us that He healed: (1) by the Word; (2) by the faith of the sick; (3) to release service; (4) to restore life; (5) to deliver from demons; (6) through the faith of others besides the sick; (7) through the faith of the desperate and persistent; (8) to reveal God (and God's heart); (9) His enemies. Therefore, we as His body must release His healing power to our generation as well.

To begin healing from bitterness, we all must purpose to do a few things:

1. Confess your bitterness as a wickedness.

It's so easy to justify our attitude when we've been hurt, but the Bible teaches that bitterness is a sin. Hebrews 12:14-15 says, "Strive for peace with everyone, and for the holiness without which no one will see the Lord. See to it that no one fails to obtain the grace of God; that no 'root of bitterness' springs up and causes trouble, and by it many become defiled..." You must seek peace with your spouse and have the grace to forgive.

2. Ask for God's strength to forgive people and diligently seek that forgiveness.

It's hard to be tender-hearted to a spouse who has hurt you, but it is possible. We have the power to forgive because Christ forgave us, and He gives us strength through the Holy Spirit.

3. Worry about changing yourself, not people.

You cannot change people—only God can. But what you can do is allow God to change your heart. If you have a log of bitterness in your own eye, how can you take the speck out of your spouse's eye? You, too, have made choices in this relationship that have hurt your spouse and the hurts need to be mended.

Even though your sister or brother's sin goes unresolved for now, he or she will answer for it one day before God (Matthew 10:26). In the same way, God will hold you responsible for the bitterness in your heart.

One of the things that I have found to be critical for any leader or husband and wife team is to have someone that they can go to in order to receive wise counsel. Believe it or not, most couples or leaders either don't have a spiritual covering, or they cannot go to their spiritual covering for several reasons. One: *Rebel spirit;* they started wrong and left their church without release.

Two: *Rejection;* they don't want their leaders to think less of them.

Three: *Pride;* they don't want to expose their shortcomings and threaten each other if they do tell someone.

Four: *Rebellion;* they don't want to submit themselves to anyone who can help them, but they have *everyone else's answer.*

True Story of an Anonymous Leader
Real Life Story/Real Lessons

A Son's Experience When His Father Falls

I know of this experience, firsthand, as my pastor-father fell hard and fast from his visible place of mega-church leadership in the early 1990s. While the eyes of the world watched pastor scandals of famed leaders on TV, I watched one of my own unfold, inside our family home.

It was difficult and painful, on every level. But with it came some rich lessons of understanding, grace, and the value of people. It brought about insight into what every tribe member should remember when the one they follow falls.

Your belief in him or her was not necessarily wrong. Often, when a leader falls from their position, those who followed him or her feel duped, setup or foolish. But while we are wise to be discerning in whom we let speak into our lives, we are always to believe the best about people. This includes leaders. Even the godliest, respected leaders can fall from their position, should they allow power, wealth, or influence to corrupt them.

You are not expected to (nor should you) take personal responsibility for them. When we choose to follow a leader, we choose to invest in their leadership. As a result, we may begin to feel like we are responsible to defend, excuse, or speak for them, taking on their fall to the point where it affects us, personally. Though we can offer our support through love and grace, it is not healthy to, in any way, own their actions.

Your response will determine your future. Because the position of a leader elicits respect, we are influenced by their actions. For a time, this may mean that we become stagnant or discouraged, doubting our ability to make wise choices or follow trustworthy leaders. But our ability to thrive depends on what we choose next. No matter who we follow that has fallen, we have the ability to move forward, choosing well for ourselves in the future.

Your realistic expectation will be important. It is vital to know several things about your fallen leader, going forward. You must know that after a time of sabbatical, the leader you have followed will likely want to lead again. You must know that he or she will feel hurt and will likely attempt to self-protect. You must remember that he or she is human and expect them to respond as such, no matter the size of their platform or how far their fall.

Your attitude toward him or her may produce change. When leaders fall, they learn to expect judgment from the watchful eyes of the world. But they long for gracious people to believe in them again. When a leader is offered grace, it provides a measure of necessary healing to their soul, which, in turn, builds their self-esteem. A tribe member who understands this can offer his or her leader a type of leadership back by spearheading a campaign of understanding and love.

131

Like any other human who suffers the loss of a valued role, when a leader falls from his or her platform, they struggle to find their place. While he or she is responsible to maintain their own integrity, it is the support members of their tribe who can help them learn to stand, again, from a very public leadership fall.

Everyone who is reading this book here is a rule that I live by. For over 28 years, right to this day, when there appears to be something that is serious to my spouse, something that she feels is overwhelming, and she's having trouble with me or something within the organization, my response is, "Who do you want to call or go and see, so this can be resolved if you believe I'm the problem."

TEN:

Faith Required to Move Forward

If the kingdom of God is going to be advanced and if Christianity is going to continue to be a force to be reckoned with in the 21st century, then it is absolutely vital that we are producing keen, "called of God" men and women who are totally in love with Jesus Christ. Why do I say this? Because it is only a strong love for Jesus that will enable us to rise above all the negatives that come against those who are truly called of God into ministry.

The Bible is full of stories of people who had to move from one place to another to align with God's plans. Abram and Sarai left their relatives in Ur; Moses had to lead the

Hebrews out of Egypt; Nehemiah had to travel from Persia to Jerusalem. In the New Testament, Peter had to go to Cornelius' house in Caesarea; Paul had to sail to Rome; and God had to scatter the disciples (see Acts 8:1) so that they would fulfill the Great Commission.

Moving forward is a decision and an act of faith. The word "forward" embodies His vision for a better tomorrow, an aspiration to be commended by one who is purposing to fight the good fight of faith. As we focus on a new beginning for our relationships, ministries and/or business future, it's helpful to understand what vehicle will be fueling this momentum for a better day for everyone.

The Lord took the opportunity to teach them about the power of faith joined to the purpose and will of God, which can do far more than instantly wither a fig tree.

In response to their bewilderment, Jesus answered and said to them, "Truly I say to you, if you have faith, and do not doubt, you shall not only do what was done to the fig tree, but even if you say to this mountain, 'Be taken up and cast into the sea,' it shall happen."

Jesus obviously was speaking figuratively. He never used His own power, nor did the apostles ever use the miraculous powers He gave them, to perform spectacular but useless supernatural feats. It was precisely that sort of grandiose demonstration that He refused to give to the unbelieving scribes and Pharisees who wanted to see a sign from Him.

Jesus had already performed countless miracles of healing, many of which they probably had witnessed. And He performed many more such miracles that they could have easily witnessed. But the sign they wanted was on a grand scale, one in which fire would come down from heaven or the sun would stand still as it had for Joshua. The literal casting of a mountain into the sea would have been just the sort of sign the scribes and

Pharisees wanted to see but were never shown.

The phrase, "rooter up of mountains", was a metaphor commonly used in Jewish literature in reference to a great teacher or spiritual leader. In the Babylonian Talmud, for example, the great rabbis are called "rooters up of mountains." Such people could solve great problems and seemingly do the impossible.

That is the idea Jesus had in mind. He was saying, "I want you to know that you have unimaginable power available to you through your faith in Me. If you sincerely believe, without doubting, it shall happen, and you will see great powers of God at work." At the Last Supper, Jesus told the Twelve, "Whatever you ask in My name, that will I do, that the Father may be glorified in the Son. If you ask Me anything in My name, I will do it" (John 14:13–14).

The requirement for receiving is to ask in Jesus' name; that is, *according to His purpose and will.* Jesus was not speaking about faith in faith, or faith in oneself, both of which are foolish and unscriptural ideas that are popular today. He was speaking about faith in the true God and in God alone, not faith in one's dreams, aspirations or ideas of what he thinks ought to be. "You ask and do not receive," James warns, "because you ask with wrong motives, so that you may spend it on your pleasures".

We must all remember, "This is the confidence which we have before Him," John says, "that, if we ask anything according to His will, He hears us" (1 John 5:14).

Mountain-moving faith is unselfish, undoubting, and unqualified confidence in God. It is believing in God's truth and God's power while seeking to do God's will. The measure of such faith is the sincere and single desire that, as Jesus said, "the Father may be glorified in the Son."

True faith is trusting in the revelation of God. When a Believer *seeks something that is consistent with God's Word* and trusts in God's power to provide it, Jesus assures him that his request will be honored, because it honors Him and His Father. When God's commands are obeyed, He will honor that obedience. And when any request is asked in faith according to His will, He will provide what is sought.

To do what God says is to do what God wants and to receive what God promises!

****

True Story of an Anonymous Pastor's Wife
Real Life Story/Real Lessons

Dear Church of Little Faith:

My husband has faithfully served you for many, many years. It has been the best of times and the worst of times. We have been through rapid growth and rapid decline, building programs, staff changes, and hundreds of weddings, funerals, and potlucks!

We have raised our kids in this church and have intentionally shielded them from many of the difficult times. We want them to love the church as Christ's body, but now that they are adults, we realize that they knew much more about the hurts and have all turned to very different churches, or no church at all.

And now, it's September and we are about to experience "National Pastor Appreciation Month". October has always felt like such a hard month for us. There is some kind of token word of appreciation, but it does not translate to the rest of the year.

We have found out that because of budget shortfalls, we will again not receive a cost of living raise. This has been the case for many years (I'm not revealing how many years without a raise, in hopes that other churches will think I am writing about THEIR church). Why are we to "trust God for our finances" but the church is not willing to "trust God for the finances needed for ministry"?

We often feel like Moses wandering in the wilderness with a multitude of griping, gossiping, and grumbling from the congregation, but thankfully, no sand or desert! If the church is doing great it is "because the members are working so hard", and if the church is struggling, it is "because the pastors are not doing enough".

We are often tired, discouraged, and feel the weight of your unrealistic expectations, your gossiping assumptions, and other negativity. BUT GOD: is faithful, true, loving, kind, encouraging, and did I mention, faithful?

When we feel the triple D's of doubt, discouragement, and despondency, God is faithful to remind us of His Delight, Dedication, and Desires. Another pastor recently asked my husband how often he has resigned in his mind, and it is often. We have sincerely and fervently asked the Lord to move us if we are the problem in our church, but we're still here. And we totally understand how so many pastors feel like they must resign and do anything else in a society that so undervalues their profession and dedication…

We have sincerely and fervently asked the Lord to move us if we are the problem in our church but we're still here. And we totally understand how so many pastors feel like they must resign and do anything else in a society that so undervalues their profession and dedication.

We are at an age that moving to a new career would be very difficult. Yet, at the same time, we long to step out in faith into the unknown. But honestly, it takes much more faith to stay with a church that likes to run the show and cannot easily trust their pastors, than to move them from an inward-focused congregation to an outward-focused, generous, unselfish congregation.

So, what's the answer? I don't know, but HE does.

The statistics about pastors giving up are frightening, but at the same time, I don't think even our best friends who know much of what we have gone through have even an inkling of the pain we have experienced.

Thanks for letting me vent – a Pastor's Wife for 30 Years. (Not an ex-pastor, but sometimes longing to be in that category.)

Pray for your leaders, because you never know what they are going through silently!

Take command of your thoughts, words, and time so that you will be in a position to take command of your destiny.

Do not be a victim. Call the shots and change your destiny. Be proactive and decisive as you declare God's Word over your life. God has given you the promise that whatsoever you declare in Jesus' name, it will be done (see John 14:13-14), so you can be all He intended you to be.

There should be no doubt in your mind that God wants to bless and prosper you. He wants you to succeed and not fail. He wants the very best for you. Remember, those who come to God must believe that He rewards those who diligently seek Him (see Heb. 11:6). This is because the one thing that pleases God is your faith.

Expect that whatever you are decreeing will come to pass. Jesus taught, "Whatever things you ask when you pray, believe that you receive them, and you will have them." (Mark 11:24).

God delegated authority to you, as a Believer, that you may accomplish His will. Inherent within this divine authority is responsibility and accountability. You are *responsible to speak in accordance with the divine will* that which has been spoken concerning you.

Kingdom authority demands that you become proactive in the establishment of purpose in your life experience. You are not to be dominated by circumstances—you are to take authority over them and decree the will of God into manifestation in the name of Jesus. After all, Jesus promised us that His

Father would give us whatever we asked in His name.

Ask the Holy Spirit to guide your words, thoughts, and faith as you take command of your day, and watch what God will do!

ELEVEN:

How to Rebuild Healthy Partnerships

Fights, arguments, and conflicts are a part of every normal relationship with family, marriage, and close working relationships. A relationship without any of these doesn't sound realistic and normal regardless of how spiritual we are.

More often than not, even simple fights could lead to breakups and breakaways from marriage and ministry. That's the sad part of fighting and allowing the enemy to get a foot in. But the good part is that every hurt or disappointment that has caused you to bleed *can be fixed*.

Let's be real; severe family conflicts without any reconciliation result in distressing experiences among those not willing to settle scores. The trauma that results may be spiritual, social, physical, material, or any combination.

Some of us come from family and church backgrounds of defeatism, divorce, pessimism, selfishness, greed, anger, addictions, and laziness. Unless we break this stronghold, these traits and tendencies may be passed on to our children or to the next ministry that we go to.

One's dysfunctional personal behavior becomes a model or example to the next generation or work environment, and the cycle can be repeated over and over again. Often, this continues until someone realizes that he or she can be the one to break the cycle and make a difference.

By developing a meaningful relationship with God, we will not only become more enriched and fulfilled, but we will also benefit many others, including our own descendants.

Most of the time, broken relationships do not get second chances even if the love is still there. Why? It's because love isn't enough to fix a broken heart or relationship, especially if the wound is really so deep that it left a big scar. On the other hand, there are relationships that deserve second chances. The difficult part is starting over again after a painful experience.

Know this, it is you and only you who can break dysfunctional traits and tendencies. And, not by trying to fix someone else ... like the kids, your spouse, the dog, your co-workers, staff or the volunteers, etc.

Let's be clear on what I am talking about here by understanding a few things.

- Dysfunctional – to interact and live in unhealthy ways; being non-productive, not constructive. Such people are not supportive, although they may intend to be.

147

- Patterns – habitual ways people interact; can be good or bad.

- Adam and Eve's Family listened to bad advice, disobeyed, blamed each other, survived through pain and toil, became angry and jealous, and committed murder.

- Abraham's Family lied about marital status (not once, but twice), had a child by Sarah's servant, showed favoritism, drove Ishmael out; Isaac lied about his marital status, showed favoritism; Jacob deceived his brother and father, was tricked by his uncle, and showed favoritism; Joseph's brothers sold him into slavery.

- David's Family had several wives and concubines, married Michal for political reasons, committed adultery, arranged for Uriah to be killed; Amnon raped his sister, Tamar, was killed by his half-brother Absalom; Absalom led a rebellion; Solomon killed his brother, Adonijah, multiplied his wives, worshipped idols; Rehoboam was harder on the people than Solomon, the kingdom was split. What a mess!

> *"Your Business Relationships & Church Family Matter to God" – Anthony McFarland*

Elements of Healthy Relationships :

1. Christ as their solid foundation.
2. Covenant Committed.
3. Emotionally mature with the help of the Holy Spirit.
4. Transforming spiritually.
5. Love and affection.
6. Communicate effectively and grow through difficulties.
7. Able to grow and change from one stage of development to another.
8. Able to cope successfully with anger and manage conflict well.
9. Able to cope with crises.
10. Able to laugh with each other.
11. Know who they are in Christ, having good self-esteem.

12. Says divorce is not an option unless one person has been extremely violent.

13. Cover each other's shortcomings

14. Maintains faith expectation over family relationships.

15. Quality time spent with each other.

16. Appropriate responsibilities.

17. A willingness to seek help when they need it.

18. Allows each person to express themselves without taking offense

19. Understanding each other's gifts and grace for the assignment

20. A servant's heart is to serve one another and those committed to their care.

Steps to Overcoming Dysfunctional Relationship Patterns

- Respect what God has said and obey Him.

- Don't always think that what you don't have means you don't have enough.

- Don't be jealous of the accomplishments of others.

- Be honest, and love even if it gets you into trouble. Do it with kindness; but be truthful.

- Face your problems and take responsibility. Own your part!

- Have a spirit of Reconciliation. Be a peacemaker with your spouse, children, and team.

- Pray, seek God's favor, His direction, and strength to break every stronghold.

- Learn to believe and trust in God when times look dark.
- Learn to resist temptation. Be faithful on purpose!
- Don't try to cover up one sin by committing another.
- Value family. When everyone else walks out the door, they will likely be with you!
- Purpose to have each other's back even in tough situations.
- Express appreciation for each other regularly.
- Learn to communicate effectively.
- Fill your home with worship and the Word. Set the atmosphere to cultivate the glory of God.
- Focus on strengths and potentials rather than weaknesses and failures.
- Learn to learn and grow through storms and attacks.
- If it doesn't work, do something different.

Here is a golden key step to mending, healing, and rebuilding relationships.

Simply put, but not as easy to do! *Forgive and forget*. It's possible to forgive yourself and others by the help and power of the Holy Spirit, although it's tough, and some would say *impossible* to forget things from the past. But even if it's hard, you need to try forgetting the painful things that happened in the past. If you do not forgive and forget, I have learned over the years that it only hurts you and sometimes others in the long run.

That's the first key on how to repair a broken relationship. Forgive the other party and start anew, and in some cases, just move on in life. Forgiveness will heal the wound, and the Holy Spirit, through prayer and worship, will stop the bleeding.

Don't bring up the things that caused conflicts in your relationship at home or at the church. But if there's a need for you to talk about the conflicts because you need to settle them, then do it for that purpose; but do not dig so deep that you will create another fight. That's why you will need the guidance and help of the Holy Spirit.

Face the problem. Don't try to run away, because you will never solve any problem if you don't face it. You need to make your partner understand every single thing about your relationship. Assess yourself and try to omit an attitude that once created conflict.

Lastly, one of the most vital components to creating a joyful, healthy, and fulfilling relationship is to *become a master at setting boundaries*. Simply put, boundaries set the space, and draws the line between where you end, and the other person begins. Creating healthy boundaries is empowering. By recognizing the need to set and enforce limits, you protect your self-esteem, maintain self-respect, and enjoy healthy relationships.

The easiest way to think about a boundary is a property line. We have all seen "No Trespassing" signs, which send a clear message that if you violate that boundary, there will be a consequence. This type of boundary is easy to picture and understand, because you can see the sign and the border it protects. Personal boundaries can be harder to define because the lines are invisible, can change, and are unique to each individual.

Personal boundaries, just like the "No Trespassing" sign, define where you end, and others begin. The boundaries are determined by the amount of physical and emotional space you allow between yourself and others. Personal boundaries help you decide what types of communication, behavior, and interaction are acceptable.

Here are elementary steps to begin setting boundaries.

Step 1: Recognize and acknowledge your own feelings.

Being able to do this is absolutely vital, because by being able to check in with ourselves and recognize how we are feeling, we have then separated ourselves from the other person.

The problem with many of us who have weak or leaky boundaries in relationships is that we become so enmeshed, so encompassed by the other person's "stuff" that we have no idea what we, ourselves, are feeling. By taking the time to break away, reflect, and really check in with yourself, you are then consciously making the distinct difference between yourself and the other person.

It seems obvious that no one would want his/her boundaries violated. So why do we allow it? Why do we NOT enforce or uphold our boundaries?

- FEAR of rejection and, ultimately, abandonment
- FEAR of confrontation
- GUILT

Awareness is the first step in establishing and enforcing your boundaries.

Step 2: Recognize how your boundaries have been crossed.

So, now looking at your feelings, stop and recognize how your boundary has been crossed. Is this person always asking to borrow money from you, but they never pay you back? Do you find yourself always answering your friend's text or phone calls late at night and it's causing you to lose sleep? Is this person always making critical comments towards you? Does this person always seem to have problems that you always have to help them with? Do you have a client who always shows up late for your appointments?

Step 3: Recognize how you need to set your boundary.

Once you can recognize what is causing you to feel overwhelmed, drained, or, simply, bad, then decide what you need to say to this person.

So, if the person is always borrowing money from you but never paying you back, then you may need to tell them that you are not letting them borrow anything else until you get paid back what you've already given. If someone keeps making critical comments towards you, then you can tell them that you don't appreciate being spoken to that way and that you will not accept it.

Step 4: Get grounded in the Word and wisdom of God.

There are two things that often happen when boundaries in relationships have been weak:

1. There is backlash from the other person and,
2. You feel guilty.

Never forget you are not responsible for the other person's reaction to the boundary you are setting. You are only responsible for communicating your boundary in a respectful manner. If it upsets them, know it is their problem. Some people, especially those accustomed to controlling, abusing, or manipulating you, might test you. Plan on it, expect it, but remain firm.

Remember, your behavior must match the boundaries you are setting. You cannot successfully establish a clear boundary if you send mixed messages by apologizing.

Step 5: Voice it!

Make your boundary known — communicate it to the other person. Keep in mind that if there is any backlash from the other person or if they want to argue, then it may be best to simply just walk away and focus on taking care of yourself. But whatever you do, don't start bleeding again. *Choose to not be the victim!*

Clinical psychologist, Margarita Tartakovsky, M.S. said, "Establishing healthy boundaries and enforcing them allows you to step into your authentic self with confidence. No one can like, love, or respect you if they don't authentically know you. And you deserve to be authentically liked, loved, and respected.

Like any new skill, energetically communicating your boundaries takes practice. If you're having a hard time with setting boundaries, "seek some support, whether [that's a] support group, another pastor, church elder, counseling, coaching or a good friend."

With whomever you choose, after you meet with them, find a friend or family member and make it a priority to practice setting boundaries together [and] in order to hold you accountable in not only setting boundaries, but resolving conflict

...IN CLOSING...

A Question We Must All Ask:
Will You Leave A Legacy or A Bloody Mess?

Presidents speak of leaving a "legacy" when their term is done. You hear expressions like: "President Clinton's legacy is..." or "What will President Bush's legacy be? ... or President Obama's?" And, of course, now everyone in the world is looking to see what effects President Donald Trump will have on this nation, and what his legacy will be. So far, it has been different from the last 49 U.S. Presidents. But we all will have to wait and see how his story will end and the legacy he will leave.

We can wonder about the impact or legacy that a particular presidency will have upon future generations. But, how about *you...* Pastor, Volunteer, King, Business person,

Apostle, Teacher, or Prophet? What do you want your legacy to be, not in man's eyes, but in God's? What spiritual blessings do you want to leave in the lives of your heirs?

This is the ultimate commentary on our leadership effectiveness. This means devoting ourselves to the development of the full potential of those around us. Think about the legacy of your leadership and how you will be remembered. Will you be remembered for your loving commitment to others? Your ability to listen? Your continual pursuit of improvement? Your consistency to walk the talk?

Most leaders don't leave a legacy. They are never mentioned again when they leave an organization, especially if they die or get fired. Then there are the ones who leave a negative legacy—a hot mess that destroys people's lives, their ministry, community or business. You know, the leader who had the going away party but wasn't invited.

However, some have powerful <u>legacies</u> that live on for years, legacies that continue to make positive impacts on people's lives, which advances the Kingdom of God and glorifies God in every sense of the word.

A commitment to God-like leadership is a commitment to personal integrity, character, and growth in Christ. Don't shortcut the process by failing to develop the needed spiritual infrastructure. More than a position, leadership is a lifestyle!

> *"The best way to leave an 'awesome' family legacy is to live for others instead of yourself"*
> *-- Rick Warren*

Here is another question to ask yourself—and it's something else to consider—if you're going to represent God in the earth realm:

Have you ever considered how God might be glorified through a shared ministry with your spouse and others? As important as her support role is, what would happen if the two of you stepped outside your comfort zone and led something together? A mission trip? A small group? A class on a subject that is close to your hearts? The possibilities are endless!

One of our marriage mentors, Pastor Jimmy Evans, in his book, *Our Secret Paradise: Seven Secrets for Building a Secure and Satisfying Marriage*, shares insights from couples he's counseled: "Marriage is about sharing. If you don't share, it's not a marriage. ... Marriage is about making decisions together. Marriage is about doing things together. What's really difficult for one person can be easy for two."

Legacies that matter are connected with people. A hundred years from now all that will matter is the people that you connected with in such a way that you added value and meaning to their lives and families. Political commentator, Walter Lippmann, said, "The final test of a leader is that he leaves behind in others the conviction and will to carry on." Ultimately, if the people you serve can't fulfill their purpose without you, you haven't been successful in raising up other leaders or making a difference in people's lives.

As my wife and I have worked diligently to develop our ministry to married couples, several beautiful things have been born. I want to share those with you, in hopes that you might feel propelled toward closer partnership with your spouse and family.

As we have role-played petty arguments and immature responses to conflict, we have better understood Paul's admonition to "conquer evil with good" (Rom. 12:21). Remember, the more we purpose to grow, God has rewarded us with spiritual growth and progress. As Timothy was told, discernable progress is essential in the ministry (1 Tim. 4:15).

Everybody says that their spouse is their best friend. That's the textbook answer, but the reality does not always reflect that response. Best friends are constantly weaving in and out of each other's worlds. They refuse to go solo.

Micheline and I are better today than when we started in ministry over 20 years ago. We see God using our gifts to help people in the body of Christ, and leaders experience victories in their lives. In addition, the church members see two people who have gone through ups and downs. They see that we have overcome the storms of marriage and ministry, and that we are laughing more, having fun, thinking together outside the box. They also sometimes see us shedding a tear as we share a heartache or a failure, because we have kept it real with one another and with everyone God brings into our lives and ministry.

Rick Warren once said, "True humility is not thinking less of yourself; it is thinking of yourself *less.*" In leadership, it can be tempting to become enamored with status. However, it is crucial that leaders focus on their staff and members more than they focus on themselves.

I have learned that the best leaders are selfless and more concerned with the well-being of others—
especially their families—than with their personal titles and ambitions. You cannot be an effective leader if you feel that you are better than your subordinates.

Let's make a decision today not to go back to broken cisterns for spiritual refreshing! Let's rediscover the value of going to the well (our Father God) rather than the stagnate, dirty cistern!! It's time to return to the Fountain of Living Waters, which brings both healing and wholeness!!!

If you can honestly say there are a few holes or a clink in your armory, humble yourself and allow God to do a NEW THING in your life, family, business and ministry this year!

Isaiah said in 43:19, "Behold, I will do a new thing; now it shall spring forth; shall you not know it? I will even make a way in the wilderness, and rivers in the desert."

167

In Closing:

Healthy leaders are spiritually and emotionally whole, rooted and grounded in relationship with God and in tune to the leading and guidance of the Holy Spirit. They lead from a place of wholeness that is expressed in Micah 6:8: "What does the Lord require of you but to do justice, to love mercy, and to walk humbly with your God?"

They are both forgiving, reverent toward God and respectful of others. This means they are willing to listen, are open to criticism and desire more to help people succeed than to punish them when they fail.

Leadership is a remarkable calling, a demanding but rewarding vocation which will ultimately come from God almighty and not people. We hope to see you one day at the finish line, we hope you finish your course healthy and whole and win your race. You're great in the eyes of God!

End Notes:

Everyone has been duly noted and given credit throughout this book in an effort for you, the readers, to reference key points from other leaders.

To schedule the McFarland's at your church, conference or special event call or write us today!

Harvest Publishing
P.O. BOX 6249
Altadena, CA 91001
1-800-282-6056